TO GOD BE THE GLORY

Personal Memoirs of
REV. W. P. NICHOLSON

With First-hand News
Accounts of the Nicholson Era

Compiled by Mavis Heaney

TO GOD BE THE GLORY

© 2004 Mavis Heaney

First Published 2004

ISBN 1 84030 151 1

Ambassador Publications,
a division of
Ambassador Productions Ltd,
Providence House, Ardenlee Street, Belfast,
BT6 8QJ, Northern Ireland.
www.ambassador-productions.com

Emerald House,
427 Wade Hampton Blvd., Greenville
SC 29606, USA.
www.emeraldhouse.com

William Patteson Nicholson

Dedicated

*To the Glory of God
and to the
Memory of Rev. W. P. Nicholson*

Also published by:
Mavis Heaney

'LISBURN – LIFE IN THE COUNTY DOWN'
(A 1950's trip down Memory Lane)   1997

FOREWORD

This book has not been 'written' as such by the author, who sees her role simply as that of facilitator in the publication of the story of Rev. Wm. P. Nicholson. In the 1950's his Personal Reminiscences were serialised in 'The Life of Faith' magazine over many months. Part I of this book is his own story, reproduced just as it was written by the evangelist himself.

Part II consists of first-hand news accounts, views and impressions written by those who recorded what they saw as events unfolded. It is hoped that these accounts of Rev. Nicholson and the great meetings empowered by the Presence of God, will bring a fresh insight as to what God can do, to those generations who have never known the experience of sitting under the ministry of Northern Ireland's most famous preacher.

As a publication, I pray that this book will be used of God to bring those outside of Christ to saving faith and that Christians might be drawn closer in their walk with the Lord. I trust that it brings back many precious memories to those who can personally recall the Nicholson era – that it will be an encouragement and incentive to all of God's people of all ages and denominations, to pray that He will once again move in His mighty power in our land as in days of yore.

May God raise up once again other 'W.P. Nicholsons' whose goal is the Glory of the Lord, and that our country will once more experience an outpouring of God's Spirit in Revival Blessing.

If my people, which are called by My Name, shall humble themselves, and pray, and seek my face, and turn from their wicked way; then will I hear from Heaven, and will forgive their sin, and will heal their land. (2 Chronicles Ch. 7 v. 14.)

To God Be All The Glory.

Mavis Heaney

CONTENTS
PART I
PERSONAL MEMOIRS

                                                          Page

Schooldays and Life at Sea 2

Wanderings Round the World,
Return to Ulster and Conversion 5

Out of the Slough of Despond 8

Experiences in Offices,
and Call to Full-time Service 11

Training in Glasgow and Belfast 14

Missions in Lanarkshire and London,
and with Chapman and Alexander 17

Riot and Revival in Lanarkshire 20

To Australia with Chapman and Alexander 23

Campaigning in Australia and America 26

A Year in Glasgow; then back to USA 29

Itinerating in Mid-West America 33

Civil War and Revival in Ulster,
Keswick and Cambridge 36

THE NICHOLSON FAMILY ALBUM 43

CONTENTS
PART II
NEWS, VIEWS, IMPRESSIONS & PERSONAL LETTERS

Page

1913   A POPULAR BANGOR EVANGELIST
Mr. W. P. Nicholson's Work
   An Interesting Study 48

1920   MISSIONS
   BANGOR – October 51

1921   MISSIONS
   PORTADOWN – May 52
   LURGAN - September 52
   NEWTOWNARDS – November 53

1922   LISBURN – UNITED PROTESTANT MISSION 54
   Orange Hall Crowded 55
   Growing Intensity of Feeling 56
   POEM: 'The Bar' 58
   'Down in the Dumps' (Words and Music) 60
   COUNSEL TO CONVERTS by Rev. W. P. Nicholson 61
   "Nicholsonians" 62
   The Lisburn Standard – Another Record Sale 63
   Evidence (of Mission Influence) 63
   'Revival in Lisburn' by Rev. N. J. Spence (Methodist Church) 63
   Tribute by Local Ministers 64

1923   RAVENHILL PRESBYTERIAN CHURCH MISSION 65
   (11th February – 11th March)
   POEM: 'The March of the Island Men' 67
   (Composed by an Island Man)
   A Memory of W. P. Nicholson by James Doggart (Canada) 68
   CARRICKFERGUS UNITED MISSION 68
   One Thousand Souls 70
   Wee Carrick 71
   ISLAND MEN AND THE MISSIONER /
   EAST BELFAST EPISODE / END OF NICHOLSON CRUSADE 72
   Great Crowds Everywhere 72
   No Use for the Choir 73
   The Albert Hall 73
   By Charabanc to Ballymena 74
   'ALBUM WITH ILLUMINATED ADDRESS' 76
   POEM: 'Rev. W. P. Nicholson's Mission' by W. Watson 81

1924   REV. W. P. NICHOLSON AT BANGOR
      Welcomed at Public Meeting 83
     MAGHERAFELT
      'Prayer availeth much' 84

1925   THE REV. W. P. NICHOLSON
      By the Very Rev. H. Montgomery, M.A., D.D. 85
     BESSBROOK C.W.U. 87
     BANGOR FAITH MISSION EASTER CONVENTION 1925
      'The Christian's Peace' by Rev. W. P. Nicholson 89
     REV. W. P. NICHOLSON TO CONDUCT MISSION
     AT BALLYNAHINCH 93
     BALLYNAHINCH MISSION 93
     A MONTH OF NICHOLSON IN BELFAST
     Mission in Assembly Hall During the Whole of August 95
     CROWDED ASSEMBLY HALL
      New Nicholson Mission / Faction and Finance Problems
      'Commercialised Religion - Fashion, Forms and Follies' 97
      Dr. Montgomery's Foreword 98
      The Origin of the Mission 99
      'Frozen with Decency' 101
      'The Cry from Macedonia' 101
     A NEW VENTURE WITH GREAT POSSIBILITIES
     Preparing the Way for an Alliance Bible School 102
     'No Slicing Up of the Bible'
     New School for Belfast / Inaugural Meeting in Y.M.C.A. 103
     Succession of the Prophets 104
     FAITH MISSION CHRISTMAS CONFERENCE 1925
      'The Worldly Church' 107

1926   THE IRISH ALLIANCE OF CHRISTIAN WORKERS' UNIONS
      Its Origins and Aims by T. Bailie (Bangor) 108
     THE WORK IN AND AROUND LONDONDERRY 110
     REV. W. P. NICHOLSON IN DERRY – January
      'Etiquette and Decorum of the Pulpit' 111
      'What is a Christian?' 112
     LONDONDERRY (Report) 114
     PORTADOWN
      Much Blessing at Portadown /
      An Example in Steadfastness and Courage 115
     CHRISTIAN WORKERS' UNION
      Success of Rev. W. P. Nicholson's Mission 116
     REV. W. P. NICHOLSON AT CAMBRIDGE
      A University Stirred 118

1926 (Continued)	**Page**

IMPRESSIONS OF NICHOLSON by a Dublin Rector 119
DEATH OF MRS NICHOLSON 121

1928 WELCOME TO REV. W. P. NICHOLSON 121
REV. W. P. NICHOLSON BACK IN THIS COUNTRY (Scotland)
    Opening of his Glasgow Campaign after a busy week
    in the North of Ireland 122

1930 'MAKING GRANNIES SING'
    Rev. W. P. Nicholson's Effort to Brighten Religion 127
    'Painless Sanctification' 127
'PACIFISM KILLED THE CHURCH'
    Rev. W. P. Nicholson's View 128
    The Recent Church Crisis 129

1931 THE LATE MRS NICHOLSON (Mother)
    Death Follows Eighteen Hours After 130

1936 RETURN OF REV. W. P. NICHOLSON
    Welcome at Ahoghill / Start of New Campaign 130

1938 REV. W. P. NICHOLSON IN RAVENHILL ROAD CHURCH
    Big Crowds Eager to Hear 132
    The Way of Salvation 133
AGNES STREET PRESBYTERIAN CHURCH 134
BANGOR CONVENTION (Faith Mission) 134
BELFAST TRIBUTE TO REV. & MRS W. P. NICHOLSON 135

1946 NICHOLSON - The Unpredictable Man by Rev. Ian R. K. Paisley 137
CARRICKFERGUS MISSION – September 139
    Salvation Army Band 139
    Ill Health 140
    Caring Touch 140
    Report – Rev. W. P. Nicholson Mission at Carrickfergus 141

1947 ENNISKILLEN
    Personal Testimony of Mr. Denzil McIlfatrick 142
(LISBURN) W. P. NICHOLSON EVANGELISTIC CAMPAIGN
DRAWS LARGE CONGREGATIONS 144
    Welcome Tea 145
    Evangelistic Campaign (Report) 146
LISBURN DISTRICT MONTHLY HOLINESS MEETING
    Large Audience Hears Rev. W. P. Nicholson's Message 147
REV. W. P. NICHOLSON'S ITINERARY 148

1949 – 1951
> LETTERS TO LISBURN
> Personally Written by Rev. W. P. Nicholson 149

1954 VETERAN ULSTER EVANGELIST IS OFF ON TOUR 159

1956 SOME APPRECIATIONS OF HIS WORK IN IRELAND 159
HILLSBOROUGH C.W.U.
> Letter from Rev. W. P. Nicholson 162
CHRISTMAS CARD 1956
From Rev. & Mrs. W. P. Nicholson 162

1957 BANGOR-BORN US RADIO EVANGELIST IS 81 TO-DAY 163

1958 BANGOR-BORN EVANGELIST IS RETURNING FROM US CAMPAIGN ... 163
> In No Doubt 165
82-YEAR-OLD NOTED EVANGELIST RETURNS TO TOUR NATIVE
ULSTER 165
THROUGH RIFLE FIRE TO MISSION
W. P. NICHOLSON AT 82 'STILL A ROUSING SPEAKER' RECALLS PAST . 166
> Tough Times 166
> Shoulder High 167
THEY QUEUE FOR AN HOUR BEFORE PRAYER MEETING 168
WORLD SINS DUE TO LACK OF PRAYER – Nicholson 169
> Hell on Doorstep 169
> Doomed 169
MISSION REPORTS
> Londonderry 170
> Lisburn 171
BELFAST WELCOME FOR REV. W. P. NICHOLSON 172
GARVAGH C.W.U. MISSION: 18th- 25th May 1958 172
ERADICATE GRUDGES CALL BY MINISTER 173
> 'No Time' 173
EVANGELIST W. P. NICHOLSON AT PORTRUSH 174
EVANGELIST HAS TO POSTPONE BELFAST MISSION 175
EVANGELIST IS 'COMFORTABLE' 175
EVANGELIST IS TO PREACH AGAIN 176
IMPORTANCE OF PRAYER STRESSED BY MINISTER 176
EVANGELIST'S LAST SERMON HERE 176
FAREWELL SERVICE FOR REV. W. P. NICHOLSON 177
NOTED EVANGELIST VISITS GARVAGH 177

1959 REV. NICHOLSON TO SETTLE IN ULSTER 178
EVANGELIST RETURNS FROM AMERICA 179

1959 (Continued)   **Page**

REV. W. P. NICHOLSON IN CORK HOSPITAL

ULSTER EVANGELIST 'CRITICAL' 179

    Improved 180

REV. W. P. NICHOLSON DIES IN CORK 180

DEATH OF REV. W. P. NICHOLSON

    Over 1,000 at Funeral Service 181

    Ordained in America 181

    Last Ulster Campaign 182

HOMECALL OF REV. W. P. NICHOLSON

    Funeral Service 183

    Graveside Service 187

BAPTIST UNION'S TRIBUTE 188

AT ASSEMBLY HALL SERVICE 188

MEMORIAL SERVICE TO THE REV. W. P. NICHOLSON AT

WELLINGTON HALL 189

MEMORIAL SERVICE – BALLYNAHINCH 189

    Memory 190

Decision Card as Used in 1859 Revival and the Nicholson Missions .. 191

POEM: 'To God Be the Glory' by Mavis Heaney 192

PHOTOGRAPHS
PART I

Cotton House, Bangor, the birthplace of William Patteson Nicholson 2

As an apprentice on the 'Galgorm Castle' 5

The 'Galgorm Castle' 5

Mrs. John Nicholson - Mother of 'W.P.' 7

The fireplace in the kitchen of Cotton House, Bangor 7

Bible Training Institute, Glasgow 14

Dr. Henry Montgomery 16

Rev. W. P. Nicholson 1920 20

Rev. W. P. Nicholson and Mrs. Nicholson with Mr. Raymond Hemmings,
Song Leader and Soloist 31

Moody Memorial Church Chicago, Illinois 32

Dr. R. A. Torrey 33

The 'Island men' who attended the meetings in their thousands 38

Keswick Convention Tent 40

The congregation exit the Keswick Tent 40

THE NICHOLSON FAMILY ALBUM

	Page

A Nicholson family gathering 44
Some of the older generation of the Nicholson family 44
W.P. with his wife and three children 45
The three Nicholson brothers, William Patteson, James and Louis 45
Cotton House near Bangor, the Nicholson family home 46
The yard and outhouses of Cotton House with family members 46

PHOTOGRAPHS
PART II

5th August 1919 – Bangor as it was just prior to the commencement
of Rev. Nicholson's Ulster ministry 50
Wm. P. Nicholson John 3.30 'Pray for me' 51
Lisburn Orange Hall 55
Railway Street Presbyterian Church, Lisburn 57
Railway Street, Lisburn 59
Ravenhill Presbyterian Church, Belfast 65
Rev. John Ross, Minister of Ravenhill Presbyterian Church 66
Rev. and Mrs. W. P. Nicholson 1920. 77
Rev. W. P. Nicholson with two senior colleagues. 80
W. P. Nicholson. 82
Faith Mission Group – Easter Convention 1925 88
C.W.U. Hall on Windmill Hill, Ballynahinch 94
Assembly Hall, Belfast 96
Interior view of the Assembly Hall 98
The Bible School at Magdalene Hall Men's Class 103
Y.M.C.A., Wellington Place, Belfast 106
A donkey bearing the 'Good News' 111
The Guildhall, Londonderry 114
Interior of 'Mary Street Cathedral', Portadown 1926 116
Grosvenor Hall, Belfast 123
Rev. W. P. Nicholson 1930 126
Rev. W. P. Nicholson 1940 136
Sloan Street Presbyterian Church, Lisburn 144
Friends' Meeting House - Railway Street, Lisburn 147
W.P. Nicholson 148
Welcome to C.W.U. Hall, Lisburn 154
Seymour Street, Lisburn c.1954 155
Rev. W. P. Nicholson 1950 158
Shankhill Road Mission, West Belfast 164
Interior View of Wellington Hall, Belfast 168

PHOTOGRAPHS
PART II

Page

Market Street, Lisburn 171
Mr. Theodore McKibbin 172
Portrush Presbyterian Church 174
Rev. and Mrs. W. P. Nicholson with their dog 'Brutus' 1958 178
The trans Atlantic liner 'Mauritania' 179
Hamilton Road Presbyterian Church, Bangor 183
The funeral cortége of the Rev. W. P. Nicholson 187
Headstone of Rev. Wm. P. Nicholson, Clandeboye Cemetery, Bangor 191
Rev. and Mrs. W. P. Nicholson 1958 photographed on their last
arrival in Ulster. 193

God give us men! A time like this demands
Strong men, great hearts, true faith and ready hands.
Men whom the lust of office does not kill,
Men whom the spoils of office cannot buy
Men who possess opinions and a will,
Men who have honour – men who will not lie,
Men who can stand before a demagogue and
Storm his treacherous flatteries without winking;
Tall men! Sun-crowned, who live above that fog
In public duty, and in private thinking
God give us men!

Quoted by Rev. James Dunlop
(Oldpark Presbyterian Church)
at the Funeral Service of
Rev. Wm. P. Nicholson
2nd November 1959

PART I

'PERSONAL MEMOIRS'

OF THE

REV. W. P. NICHOLSON

Schooldays, and Life at Sea

Adventure as a Cadet on a Sailing Ship

Everything in this world of ours, and everybody in it, has had a beginning, sometime, somewhere. It is therefore fitting and proper, in these reminiscences, to begin at the beginning. If I didn't do this you might think I was hardly a human being like yourself, and therefore all my experiences would not be applicable to you.

I was born on April 3, 1876, a few miles out of Bangor, Co. Down, N. Ireland. I have heard since that there was a difference of opinion about the date, between my mother and a maiden aunt. My maiden aunt firmly declared that I was born on April 2nd, and not on the 3rd. My dear mother would have none of it. She always held to it that I was born on the 3rd. That settled it forever. I have sometimes wondered whether her superstitions about April 1st biased her and made her stick to the 3rd. She may have been a wee bit frightened. I might be the same as the day, "Fool's day." I am glad it was settled. I have never had the shadow of a doubt about the fact of my birth, and date. I know for sure, not hope, I am or think I am, but dead sure about it. I have every evidence I am alive; also I feel sure the date is right too. You say, "What makes me sure of the date"? I have the word of my dear mother, and I am sure she wouldn't lie to me about it. She was a sweet sinner saved by grace, and told the truth about it.

Cotton House, Bangor, where William Patteson Nicholson was born
The lady at the gate is his cousin Jane (Jinny) Campbell

Sea Fever

Years after we all moved to Belfast, so that we children could have good schooling. We were put into the Model School, where we were taught clearly, and painfully at times, all we needed. They were old-fashioned and believed not only in moral suasion, but in the propulsive power of a new affection, viz., a good sally rod, well seasoned. I have warm recollections of this new affection. I am sure I needed it. I would have lost something if I hadn't had it.

About this time I had a bad dose of the sea fever. I became restless and discontented, and wanted to go to sea and become a sailor. I played truant from school and spent days around the docks looking at the ships and longing to get away in one of them. Those were the days of the Golden Age of sailing ships. When my parents found me out and heard me say that I wanted to go to sea, they tried to change me, by letting me leave school and go to business.

I was put into a linen merchant's office. It was alright for a time, but I was soon as bad with the sea fever as ever. They gave in to me, and I became a cadet, bound for four years. My parents had to pay a premium for the privilege, and I received no wages. I will never forget the day I had my new suit on, with the brass buttons on it, and my cap with its gold badge on it. We sailed away soon after.

It was a hard and harsh training. It either made you or broke you. Yet I loved it, especially up aloft during a gale of wind – the wind shrieking through the rigging, and the ship rolling from side to side; the seas like miniature mountains. It intoxicated me. Food was scarce – tough salt beef and salt pork and Liverpool pantiles for biscuits. The regular hours, fresh air and hard work and instant obedience made you healthy, if mostly unhappy.

Unforgettable Voyage

I shall never forget one voyage. We were loaded with Northumberland coal, bound for the West Coast of South America. The cargo went on fire when we were off the East Coast of South America. We managed to put it out by digging in the coal. We rounded Cape Horn, and a week or so later we were caught in a regular N. Easter. We had to hove to for days, under lower topsails and fore staysail. The sea was mountainous and cold. The wind veered to the S. West, and we had to wear the ship round – a very trying experience in such a sea and so little sail. She tossed and rolled as if she would go under. The cargo began to shift. I remember that it was my watch at the wheel from 10.00 p.m. to 12.00. Of course the wheel was lashed, but someone was always at the wheel. The ship began to list badly. Around midnight she was almost on her side. The helm was out of the water. We couldn't steer her. We tried to ease her by cutting off the topgallant masts. We cut the stays, but they bent like a cane, yet wouldn't break off. We had to cut the topmast stays and the mast cracked like a clay pipe stem. We couldn't get rid of all this wreckage because it was under the lee side under water. Twenty-eight men were clinging on the upper side all that night, wet, cold, half frozen.

Early morning we saw a vessel coming our way, going before the wind at great speed. She soon saw us and hove to, and put off a lifeboat with nine men in it. She came as near to us as she could; she couldn't come too near because of the wreckage all around us. They called on us to jump overboard, and they would pick us up. What could we do? We couldn't jump, we were stiff. We hadn't had a bite for over twenty-four hours. If we could have jumped in such a sea we would never have reached a boat. We couldn't even shout. The lifeboats stayed by as long as they could, but when they saw we were not moving, they turned back to their ship and squared their yards and sailed away.

Terror of Death

Our feelings were indescribable. Hope seemed all gone. We were all filled with despair. If ever I prayed to God to save me – not from shipwreck; that never entered my head – but save me from hell, it was then. Oh, it was real. All my boasted infidelity and scorn of religion was gone. I knew that if we were to sink I would not only be in a watery grave, but a burning hell. The fear of hell filled me with terror. I had cursed God and sinned against Him grievously and wilfully. When it comes to a time like this, all the doubts and denials and defiance vanish from you, and you know the reality of hell and having to meet God. Laughter and mockery depart, like the ass Absalom was riding on when caught by the hair in the branches of a tree.

I noted that all the other men were feeling as I was. We were like rats caught in a trap. Like cowards we were squealing for mercy. The God we had defied and denied we were now crying to for mercy. I promised Him if He would save me and rescue me from drowning I would serve Him. As I look back now to that time, I tremble with fear, because as I cried to God, a queer calm came over me, and all fear of hell and judgement passed away. I said to myself, if we are not saved from drowning my soul is saved from hell.

It was a delusion of the devil He had filled me with a false peace. If I had been drowned I would have gone to hell deluded and damned. Because after we were rescued, I continued in sin. I again denied and blasphemed God. I gave myself up to wickedness and debauchery. I laughed at my fears when so near death. Friends: let me warn you who are unsaved. You think you can live in sin and die in peace, and go to heaven. If the devil can deceive you now, while you are in health of body and mind, do you think he can't deceive you when dying? If he can give you peace now while in health, how much more will he deceive you when you are weak and sick and dying? Be not deceived. "God is not mocked." You can't make a convenience of God, and think you can be saved when you like. Only *now* is the accepted time. *Now* is the day of salvation. Tomorrow is but another day. Tomorrow is *Eternity*.

You may wonder how we were saved. We broke into the hold and shifted the cargo over to the other side until we got the vessel over so that we could use the helm. We rigged up some sail on what was left of the masts, and turned back round Cape Horn. There we were picked up by a British small warship, and towed into Stanley Harbour, Falkland Islands. We jury rigged her there and sailed for home to be fitted out again.

As an apprentice on the 'Galgorm Castle,'1891-96

The 'Galgorm Castle'
Courtesy of Harland & Wolff

Wanderings Round the World, Return to Ulster, and Conversion

The days of my slavery and servitude as an apprentice on a sailing ship were ended while we were at sea, so the first port we arrived at viz. Cape Town, South Africa, I demanded my release, which was granted. I arrived in a strange land and a large city without a friend or a penny of money. If ever there was a lonely, home-sick man, it was me. I walked up the main street, and to my astonishment I met a young fellow who had cleared out of a ship the voyage before. He was from a town near Bangor. Maybe I wasn't glad!

Sowing Wild Oats

He got me a job on the Railway as a porter. That was the only job I couldn't do, and wouldn't do. My pride was too tender to allow me to continue, so I made my way up country on the Cape to Cairo railway construction. They were glad to get men; men were scarce, for so many died of blackwater fever. They said that every sleeper on the railroad was a white man's grave.

Life was wild and wicked. All restraint was cast away. Most men were living under assumed names. I was as wild as the rest, but never was free from conviction of sin. As I saw so many dying of the fever – twenty-four hours after they were stricken, they died – I was continually filled with secret dread and terror. In fact, it became unbearable. I felt I would have to be saved if I stayed there any longer. So Satan told me to leave and go South on the railroad, and I could become a Christian. No one would know me. If I became a Christian (he told me) here, I would be jeered and sneered at.

So off I went 1,800 miles away. When I arrived at the town I had decided on, who should I meet but an old shipmate. That ended my becoming a Christian. How cute and subtle the old devil is. My convictions increased, and I could find no rest, peace or satisfaction. So I journeyed north again. While there a friend of mine became deadly sick. There wasn't a doctor within a hundred miles. The heat was terrific. I sat at his bedside fanning him and caring for him during the night.

He was delirious. Raving about his mother and boyhood days and home. Toward morning he seemed to be sinking. He wakened up and looking at me, said, "Billy, I can't die, I am not saved. Could you help me?" What could I say? I wasn't saved myself and was soaked in liquor at the time. He cried out "O God, if you make me well, I will become a Christian and serve Thee." The amazing thing was that the crisis of the fever passed in his favour, and he got well. This made me more anxious and miserable than ever. A doctor arrived some time after and told him he must clear out, for he couldn't live in that climate. He told me this, and suddenly asked me if I would come home with him. With hardly a thought I said, yes. So I gave in my notice and lifted my money, and we started for Cape Town en route home, by steamer to Southampton.

When we were nearing the port I began to wonder how I would be received at home. I had caused them much sorrow and shame by my sinful, wilful wandering. They hardly knew where I was. They never dreamed I was coming home. I wondered, would they kill the prodigal instead of the calf? I wired I had arrived and was coming home. They couldn't believe it was from me, and sent the wire to another family of the same name. When we were crossing over by steamer to Belfast, I wired again; and when I arrived at Belfast I wired that I was coming by 11 p.m. train to Bangor. But I made the mistake putting the time of my arrival as 11 *p.m.* instead of 11 a.m.

A Mother's Welcome

When I arrived at Bangor there was no one to meet me. I felt like turning back again. But I thought, while I am here I might as well take a look at the old home. So I made my way there. I passed by the driveway to the home several times, and just as I was making up my mind to go away, my dear old mother came out of the home to cross the drive with a basket of washing to put on the clothes line to dry. I couldn't help myself, I said, "Mother." She looked up and saw me, dropped the basket and had me in her arms in no time. My tears and hers blended, as she kept saying, "Oh, I am so glad to see you." Over and over again, she hugged me, and loved me, and wept over me. Not a word about my sin or sinful life. Just glad I was home.

Three weeks passed by when one Monday morning I was sitting by the fire reading the morning paper and smoking, while mother was busy preparing the breakfast. Suddenly, and without warning, a voice said to me, *"Now or Never."* You must decide or reject Christ." Sweat broke out on my brow. I trembled all over with fear. In my heart I cried "Lord, I yield. I repent of all my sin and now accept Thee as my Saviour."

Mrs. John Nicholson
Mother of 'W.P.'

Suddenly and powerfully and consciously, I was saved. Such a peace and freedom from fear, such a sweet and sure assurance filled my soul. I turned to my mother and said, "Mother, I am saved." She looked at me and nearly collapsed and said, "When?" I said, "Just now." "Where?" "Here, where I am sitting." She cried with joy unspeakable. She couldn't say a word, but just hugged me and cried. Her baby boy had not only come home, but was now saved.

The fireplace in the kitchen of Cotton House

Converted . . . But . . . !

Happy day, happy day, when Jesus washed my sins away! It was on a Monday at 8.30 a.m. the twenty-second day of May, 1899. What a day. A day that will never see an end. I wired to my brother in Edinburgh, Scotland. He was a medical student, and he took his F.R.C.S. (Edin.) there and went to the John G. Paton mission to the South Sea cannibals. I wired, "I have decided for Christ!" Maybe he wasn't glad, and let me know it!

Isn't it wonderful the way the Lord leads us? He works in a mysterious way His wonders to perform. His ways are past finding out, but they are perfect. Hallelujah! When He sets His love on you, He will never give up. He will never grow weary seeking to save us, until He brings us to Himself, crying, "I yield. I yield. I can hold out no longer. I sink by dying love compelled, and own Thee Conqueror."

"O Love that wilt not let me go, I rest my weary soul on Thee; I give Thee back the life I owe, that in Thine ocean depths its flow may richer, fuller be." What a wonderful Saviour is Jesus my Lord!

The peace and joy and assurance continued, but in a fluctuating way. Sometimes doubting, sometimes trusting, sometimes joyful, sometimes sad. All grosser sins dropped off me, and I had no sorrow about it, or any bother with them; but the sins of the flesh and the spirit continued to plague me greatly. Envy, jealousy, malice, hatred. I could crush them down, but they continued to rise up again, more vigorous than ever.

The fear of man was a dreadful snare, and I was helplessly caught by it. I was ashamed of Christ, and ashamed of being seen with out-and-out Christians. I was a sneak and a coward, if ever there was one. I despised myself, but was helpless about it. The fear of what men would say and do, if I confessed Christ, terrified me.

I attended church twice every Sunday, and joined the men's Bible class. I read my Bible, but didn't get any good out of it, and had little or no desire for it. Prayer was a real penance, and seemingly useless. What a wretched, miserable experience I was passing through. If I could have given it all up, I believe I would have done so. I wondered was this all that salvation meant? So many saved ones around seemed to be *enjoying* the same experience as myself. We never heard there was any way out, from the preaching. It was "Do the best you can." "Hitch your wagon to a star." "Each victory will help you," but I rarely, if ever had victory. I always enjoyed living even in sin, but since I was saved, I was spoiled for living in sin, but wasn't enjoying it. "O wretched man that I am, who shall deliver me from the body of this death?"

Out of the Slough of Despond

I lived in this distracted state for nearly seven months after my conversion. Some have told me I wasn't converted at all – that I only thought I was. But they were wrong. I was truly born again, and a new creature in Jesus Christ. I had the inward witness clear, and the outward evidence that I was a changed man. The Spirit answered to the Blood and told me I was born of God. He is the Spirit of truth, and would never deceive me by lying to me. I hated sin, but was continually overcome by it. I loved holiness, and longed to be perfectly whole, but never experienced it. I was truly a child of God, but a slave of the devil. My life was up and down, but more down than up. I was committing sin and confessing it, but rarely having victory over it. I believed there was deliverance for me, but how to obtain it, I didn't know.

Dissatisfied and Defeated

I knew some Christians who were living a victorious, joyous, soul-winning life. How I envied them! I am sure if I had only made known to them the fluctuating, failing kind of life I was living, they would have led me into the open secret; but I was ashamed to make my experience known. What a wretched state I was in. I had left the world and worldlings, and come to Christ as my Saviour. But He was a root out of the dry ground. He had no form nor comeliness, no beauty that I should desire Him. I was dissatisfied, discontented and defeated, and there seemed no way out for me.

I could not enjoy the world and its pleasures, and I was not enjoying the pleasures at God's right hand. The world renounced had left an aching void, but my salvation didn't seem to fill the void. I am glad, in a way, that I had to pass through this long seven-month experience, because I have helped so many believers who were living the same sort of life, out into a life of holiness, happiness and helpfulness. God never intended His people to live wandering in the wilderness. He brought them out of Egypt, by blood and power, to bring them into Canaan.

Thank God, the day of my deliverance was at hand. One of the leading businessmen of the town, an out-and-out man for Christ and souls, arranged for a "Convention for the deepening of the Christian life." He was Mr. S. G. Montgomery, brother of Dr. Henry Montgomery. The Rev. J. Stuart Holden was to be the speaker. He and my brother James were close friends in their student days, working in connection with the C.C.S.M.

I was invited to attend. I didn't know what sort of a meeting the convention was. I thought it first to be another religious service; so had no fear about attending. What a surprise I got the very first meeting, as I heard Mr. Holden speak. It seemed to me that my brother, or some one, had told him about the failure I was as a Christian. I felt a little annoyed. But I was there the next night, and I felt sure he had been told about me, for he made clear and public my spiritual condition. I was more annoyed than ever, and determined I wouldn't attend another meeting.

I was there again the next night, however, when it was made clear to me that Jesus had made full provision for not only my Salvation, but for a life of victory over the world, the flesh and the devil. As I had received Jesus Christ as my Saviour, by repentance and faith, not of works or merit or desert, but on the ground of grace and by faith, so if I would surrender fully, laying my all on the altar of sacrifice, and receive by faith the Holy Spirit to sanctify me and fill me, He would give me a clean heart and possess me fully; and as I continued to walk in the light as He was in the light, that is, walk by faith and obedience, the Blood of Jesus Christ His Son would keep on cleansing me from all sin.

Deceits of the Devil

It was all so sublimely simple. I was amazed. I thought it could only be attained by hard work, whereas it was an obtainment. The gift of the Holy Spirit. I didn't immediately obtain it. I was frightened to make the surrender without any strings attached. It was this "unconditional" surrender that filled me with fear, and hindered me receiving the blessing. The devil was working overtime with me, filling me full of mostly lies. He told me I would have to be a missionary, to leave all and go abroad; or I would have to make a fool of myself in some public way. I would lose my reputation, etc.

The Salvation Army had come to our town. The Corps was two wee girls in uniform. They held open-air meetings and made a noise with their tambourines. Their first soldier was a man called Daft Jimmy. He had hardly enough brains to give him a headache, but he had sense enough to get saved. He carried the flag as they marched the streets. On his jersey, a red one, he had the women put by white yarn these words on his back, "Saved from public opinion." I was told by Satan that I would have to go to the open-air meeting and march down the street with two wee girls and a fool. Maybe this didn't fill me with a horrible dread. I would be laughed at by all my friends. I would lose my reputation.

Unconditional Surrender

I said, "Lord, I will be willing to go to Timbuctoo or Hong Kong, or even die decently as a martyr." I couldn't get out of it, I became more and more miserable and, oh, so hungry for freedom and victory. At last I became desperate. The last night of the convention I saw it was a clean-cut, unconditional surrender, or continue wandering in failure, defeat and dissatisfaction. I left the meeting and went down to the shore, and there under a clear sky and shining stars I made the complete, unconditional surrender. I cried out, "Come in. Come in, Holy Spirit. Thy work of great blessing begin. By faith I lay hold of the promise, and claim complete victory o'er sin."

Hallelujah! What a thrill, what a peace, what a joy. Although an old-fashioned Presbyterian I began to weep and sing and rejoice like an old-fashioned Free Methodist. When I came home, I told my mother, "The surrender has been made, and I am free and so happy." She was delighted, for she told me she wondered whether I was really saved or not. She knew the blessing, for she had received it under the Rev. Andrew Murray's preaching held in a convention in Belfast.

The wonder to me was, that all the fear of what men might say or do had vanished, and now I was willing to do anything or go anywhere. The very thing I dreaded most, before receiving the blessing, about the Salvation Army meeting, was faced. I couldn't say I was very happy about it. But I told the Lord I would do what He wanted, cost what it may. So I went to their open-air meeting on a Saturday night, when the country people are all in and mostly everybody is out shopping or meeting friends on the street. Any other night of the week the streets were largely deserted. I tried to compromise about the day, but He held me to Saturday.

As I walked down the street that Saturday it seemed as if every friend and relative I ever had were out and about. When I came to the open-air meeting and saw the two wee Salvation Army girls singing and rattling their tambourines, and poor Daft Jimmy holding the flag, I nearly turned back. Talk about dying. I was dying hard that night; I stepped off the footpath and stood in the ring. The soldiers looked at me. Then to my horror one of them said, "The people don't seem to stop and listen: let us get down on our knees and pray." What could I do? I couldn't run away. So down I got on my knees.

The crowd gathered around. I could hear their laughter and jeers. The officer prayed a telegram prayer - short and to the point. I could have wished the prayer had been as long as the 119th Psalm. I stood up, blushing and nervous. They got the collection while the crowd was there and then to my horror, she said "Brother! Take this tambourine and lead the march down the street to the Barracks." I couldn't let a girl beat me, so I took it. That did it. My shackles fell off and I was free. My fears all gone. I started down the street, whether in the body or out of the body, I can't tell. I lost my reputation, and fear of man: joy and peace and glory filled me. I can see now, and understand why the Lord dealt with me so drastically. I would never, I believe, have come right through and out-and-out for Christ, in any other way. I was naturally timid and shy. I lost something that night I never want to find again, and I found something I never want to lose. That is, I lost my reputation and fear of man, and found the joy and peace of the overflowing fullness of the Spirit. Hallelujah!

Oh, the peace my Saviour gives,
Peace I never knew before;
And my way has brighter grown,
Since I learned to trust Him more.

Experiences in Offices, and Call to Full-time Service

John tells us (John 10: 10) that Jesus came to give life, and – "more abundantly." Every born again one has life, but comparatively very few know the abundant life experimentally. It is this abundant, abounding, overflowing life that is the birthright of every born again one. Satan moves earth and hell to keep Christians from going in for it. He does his level best to hinder a sinner coming to Christ; but when he fails to do this, he works harder than ever to hinder them becoming candidates for the blessing, and possessing it.

Joy of Full Salvation

Well, he knows they will never do his work much hindrance or harm by merely having life. He knows also that when they possess the abundant life they are completely spoiled for worldly pleasures and find all their joy and entire satisfaction in Jesus Christ alone. By their abundant life of overflowing love, joy, peace, power and victory, they are commending and recommending Jesus Christ to others. This does more to hinder him keeping sinners from being saved, and helps and encourages and entices them to accept Jesus Christ as their Saviour.

Oh, the joy of full salvation. Oh, the peace of love divine. Why is it that so many saved ones are prejudiced and suspicious of the blessing? They will never know true peace and satisfaction until they possess it. What a change it wrought in my life. I had no difficulty in witnessing for Christ, in meetings and to individuals. I began holding meetings in the homes, especially working men's kitchens. They would gather around a big peat fire, with an oil lamp on one side. There I stood before the fire and the lamp. If I hadn't inspiration I had perspiration.

One of the first meetings I held, I was sure I had a great sermon; but when I started to speak, all I had prepared vanished and I stood dumb. One dear old lady called out, "Never mind, Mr. Nicholson, you'll do better the next time."

There was no further talk about my leaving home again. I got work in the Railway freight department, invoicing. I didn't know a thing about invoicing. Maybe I didn't pray about it. I soon was as fast and accurate as any of them. There were about a dozen of us invoicing, but none were saved. I wondered how I could speak to them about their souls' salvation. The Lord gave me the idea to help them in their work. Some were slow because they were lazy or careless. After I would give them an hour or so, they couldn't very well not listen to my testimony.

I went round each one frequently. They were quite willing to listen to me under the circumstances. I never had the joy of leading one of them to Christ. The Lord was watching my interest all the time I was busy about His work. I received a note on my desk one morning, telling me the head of the department wanted to see me in his private office, at 11 a.m. The old devil filled me with fear because I was interfering with his men, etc. I went to his office on time. He told me there was a good job, and more pay, in a shipping company's office. He said he had influence there, and could get me the job. I wondered why he chose me. Was it to get rid of me? Had I not been doing good work?

I thanked him, and then said, "Sir, would you mind telling me why you were interested in me to do this? I hadn't been a year in the office. Other clerks had been there many years." He said, "I noticed how you went round every department learning their work, so that when any clerk was absent you were able and willing to do their work as well as your own." He said that he was determined to help me on, as I was ambitious and industrious. I told him that my reason for doing as I did, was that I wanted to win them for Christ. He was flabbergasted. I had a good chance for a word with him about his soul, but didn't succeed in winning him for Christ.

Tables Turned

The next office I was in, there were twenty or more in it. I was put in the accountants department. I didn't know the first thing about such work, but I was eager and willing to learn. The head of the department was a very bad cursing, swearing foul-mouthed sinner. I rebuked him. It made him mad. I couldn't understand why I received 10s. rise weekly, but some time afterwards I discovered why.

I had come by train to work, as I did every day. This day while reading my Bible in the train a verse got hold of me, "No weapon that is formed against thee shall prosper: and every tongue that shall rise against thee in judgement thou shalt condemn. This is the heritage of the servants of the Lord and their righteousness is of me, saith the Lord." (Isaiah 54: 17). I couldn't tell you how that gripped me. During the day one of the clerks I had led to Christ, came to me and said, "Do you know how you got the 10s. rise some time ago?" I said "No." He told me that my boss went to the Managing Director and told him I didn't know anything about accountancy. It wasn't fair that such a one should be put in his department. The Director asked him only one question "Is he lazy?" "No," said my boss, "he isn't lazy; I can hardly keep him in work. As long as I explain the work to him, he does it, and is asking for more." The Director said, "Give him 10s. rise and keep him in your department." When I heard this, maybe my heart didn't sing and praise God.

Widening Horizons

When I had the chance, I came to my boss and said, did he wonder why I wasn't fired but got a rise of 10s? He said he did. I opened my Bible and told him to read Zechariah 2: 8, which he did. I said to him he was touching the apple of God's eye when he was trying to injure me. It put a fear in him, and he was different afterwards.

From these experiences I learned the truth of the promise, "Seek *first* (not second or third) the kingdom of God, and His righteousness; and all these things shall be added unto you." It always pays to serve and love the Lord Jesus. When we put our all, and all our affairs, into His hands, and leave them there, they are safe from all harm and injury. The worst of it is in so many cases we leave everything with Him, but only for a while. Then we undertake our own affairs, and as a result we make an awful mess of things, bringing pain, loss and misery to us. Oh, what peace we often forfeit. Oh, what needless pain we bear, all because we do not carry everything to God in prayer (and leave it there).

I felt a change was coming in my life. I didn't know when or how, but I knew the time would come for me to go out into full-time service. The Rev. J. Stuart Holden and I spent several hours together one day while he was over in Ulster. He told me he was sure I would be out in Christian work, but "Don't be in a hurry. Wait on God, until you are sure, and a door is opened." I didn't tell him I felt the same about my future. I thought it might seem presumption on my part.

All the time I was free from the office, I was holding meetings, speaking in the open-air, and giving out tracts. Every Sunday I held a meeting in a wee Orange Hall in a village a few miles from Bangor. I visited every home every Sunday before the service, inviting them to come to my meeting. I prayed with everyone who would allow me, and left a Spurgeon sermon. One dear old lady sitting at the door of her thatched cottage, when asked to come to my service, said "God love you, Mr. Nicholson, I don't need to go because you speak so loud the whole village can hear you." My seafaring life gave me a good voice, so when I got warmed up preaching, you could hear me a mile away or more. It annoyed some.

The door opened for me to prepare myself for full-time service for God. I don't remember how it all came about, but the door was unmistakably opened, I couldn't have refused and kept in close communion with my Lord and Saviour. The men in the office were sorry to see me leave, and wished me every success in my new field of service. Even the boss who tried to have me fired, and got me a rise of wages instead, was more than sorry to see me leave. I have wondered whether they were sorry because they mightn't get one to fill my place, who would give his time and service helping them, as I did. God makes the wrath of men to praise Him, if we only give Him a chance.

Training in Glasgow and Belfast

Bible Training Institute, Glasgow

The change had taken place. I said goodbye to clerking, and entered the Bible Training Institute, Glasgow, as a student.

I have vivid memories of my first few days there. I have always suffered from shyness. Even yet, after fifty years in the ministry, I am afflicted by it every time I enter a pulpit or step on a platform. After I arrived at the Institute I was shown my wee cubicle, containing a single bed, a chair, a table and a dresser. I liked having a private room. The idea of a crowded dormitory was a terror. I was so shy I couldn't face coming to the dining room and meeting all the students, so I fasted and prayed. That day I didn't appear at any meals. I slipped out to a lunch counter instead. A student was sent to my room to see if I was sick. He saw how I felt, and took me in charge. As I met my first experience with the staff and students around the dining table, I soon felt at home.

Student Experience

I enjoyed myself at the Institute, but found it hard work at first to pay attention to the lectures and take notes, and especially the study periods in my room. A seafaring, free and easy sort of life didn't make for student habits.

The Bible was our only book for study. What a treasure it became, as day by day we sat under the teachers as they expounded it to us. Then great men were brought in to lecture, including Professors Denny, Orr, and Lindsay. Ministers were brought to us. I especially remember Dr. Alexander Whyte, of Edinburgh. What an inspiration and education it all was to me.
I was greatly surprised how soon some of the students who had come to the Institute on fire for God and souls, soon allowed their fire to die down. This was specially seen at the morning half hour devotions following united family worship led by the Principal. A few verses were read, then open prayer for all who desired to engage. At the beginning of the session, many were eager to engage in prayer, but by and by very few would pray. The pause was very embarrassing.

Some of us arranged to ease the situation. This caused me to wonder, but I found out the cause. They were depending on, or substituting, the lectures we were receiving, for private devotions. We were awakened every morning by an electric bell ringing on every floor. We were supposed to rise and spend thirty minutes in private devotion before family worship in the classroom. Many seemed to sleep after the first bell, however, instead of rising for Bible reading and prayer, then they rushed down to family devotions. No wonder prayer died down.

I tried to help them in this. After the first bell rang, I got hold of a dust pan and brush and went along the corridors, banging the dust pan. The noise was very disturbing, and many were very annoyed. I determined if they wouldn't rise, they wouldn't be allowed to sleep. The response to my efforts was varied and loud, and not altogether orthodox.

I was always getting into trouble, one way and another. I seemed to be breaking six rules to keep one. I remember getting into serious trouble with the Matron. She was a fine English lady, but somehow she couldn't quite understand the Scotch or the Scotch-Irish, i.e. men from Ulster. Especially me. We had to write about anything we needed for our room, and sign our name and room number. I wrote her one day about something, and after signing my name, I put Amos 4: 11. I was called to her office. She asked me why I insulted her. I said, "How?" She told me to read the Scripture I had in my letter. I was told to read verse 2. I read it to her to my horror. "The Lord God hath sworn....that He will take you away with hooks, and your posterity with fish hooks." I nearly burst out laughing, but I managed to say that I didn't mean verse 2, but verse 11. I read it to her, saying it was my testimony. "Ye were as a firebrand, plucked out of the burning." She let me off, but I felt she didn't forgive me.

Open-Air Witness

What a grand time I had speaking at Bible conferences, Bible classes, Sunday services in the churches in the country, as well as in the city. I don't believe there was a city like Glasgow for Gospel preaching, and all sorts of meetings. Open-air meetings were everywhere, especially on Saturdays and Sundays. What marches we had through the streets, shouting and singing as we marched, carrying sandwich-boards front and back, with Scripture on them. We had all sorts of trumpets and concertinas. Some had torches, some a drum. I loved carrying a drum. The last time I carried one I got so happy I put the drumstick through the old drum.

The Saturday night meetings were usually provided with tea. As you entered you were handed a cup and a poke, i.e. a paper bag with some pastry in it. When the meeting was convened, the workers came round with big tea kettles with tea sugared and milk. Choirs sang. Solos were rendered. Then we had a magic lantern. They had none of the modern movie machines: just slides. The lecture would be Bunyan's Pilgrim's Progress, the Prodigal Son, the Passover, or some story with conversion in it. What soul-saving meetings they were!

Dr. Henry Montgomery

Inspiring Leaders

When Monday came round I was always as hoarse as any raven. What a crowd of men they were who took charge of these meetings – Peter McRostie, Sandy Galbraith, Robert Logan; evangelists such as Durn Thompson Jr., etc., etc. There were giants in those days. Leading commercial princes like Lord Overton, Lord Maclay, Sir John Campbell, shippers like the Sloans and ship builders like Napier and many others. They were not merely figure heads: they were out and out evangelistic men, preaching in the open air as well as in mission halls and church services.

What a time we had in our Homiletics sessions. One student was selected to preach. The text was given as you reached the platform. You were given three minutes to preach. I was selected one session, and the text given me was Zechariah 1: 5, "Your fathers, where are they?" My heart was shaking like a lamb's tail when drinking its mother's milk. Sweat broke out on my brow. My knees were knocking their brains out. When I stood up before the class my mind became blank. I gave out the text, "Your fathers, where are they?" I said I didn't know. I didn't know who they were, when they were born, or where they were born, or who their parents were, how they lived, or where and when they died. But I was sure of this one thing, viz. If they were saved they were in heaven; but if they were not saved, they were damned and in hell. I sat down in great silence; then they burst out laughing. I was never selected again.

During the mid-summer I became assistant to Dr. Henry Montgomery, at the Albert Hall, Belfast. What a time I had. I got an insight into an evangelistic ministry, and practical experience in doing it. I have never seen such a man as Dr. Montgomery. Night and day, in season and out of season, indoor and outdoor, wherever a crowd was gathered, he couldn't pass it by. He would get a box or chair from a nearby home, and up he would get, urging men to repent and believe. When he was done, I was told to get up and do my best. When the factory workers were getting out, after their day's work, he would get a kitchen chair and preach. It took preaching with simplicity and Holy Ghost power, to hold men and women who were on their way home. He said to me, "If you can't hold them, you haven't much of a message and you are not fit to preach."

Memorable Vacation

The open-air meetings on Saturday evenings were held often to after midnight, when the pubs were closing and the drunks were put out. The meetings were lively and stormy, but many were saved. Dr. Montgomery was well known all over the city; much beloved and bitterly hated. You could tell what kind of people they were by their attitude toward him. He had left a large and flourishing congregation and large salary, to go among the working class district; and there he erected a large building and built up a large congregation. Souls were continually being saved. Old people were cared for by sending them to the seaside for a week or two. Mothers and their babies were sent to the country for change, rest and health.

It was a wonderful summer for me. It gave me a passion to win souls for Christ, and conduct all kinds of meetings and make them attractive and successful. I was tired when I returned to B.T.I.

Missions in Lanarkshire and London, and with Chapman and Alexander

It was good being back again in the Bible Training Institute, and meeting the students once more. I hadn't any difficulty about meeting them again. My shyness didn't prevent me feeling at home among them. It was becoming easier to study, and the many meetings, held here and there, every week, helped to relieve the monotony, and keep me from getting dried up.

The days of preparation soon were ended, and I was faced with the question of what was God's directive will for my future in His service. I had received several "calls" to work, but couldn't see and feel clear, until the call came to become an evangelist for the Lanarkshire Christian Union. Then I felt sure this was His will for me. Several shires (or counties, as they are called in N. Ireland) in Scotland have an evangelistic committee, composed of leading businessmen and ministers of all denominations. They engage an evangelist, who labours in that shire all the year round.

Lanarkshire has the highest population in Scotland. It is the coal and steel centre in Scotland - something like Pittsburg, U.S.A. Missions were held all winter in churches and halls. During the summer I had a large tent. The workers and congregations were coal miners and steel workers. I did enjoy the work among them. The workers were mostly red hot, out and out daredevils for the Lord and souls. We were not bothered about our reputations, or what men said or did to us. We had been delivered from the fear of what men said or did. We had no reputation to consider, because we had lost it.

Riot or Revival

When we began a mission in a town or village, we weren't there long before we had either a riot or revival. Sometimes we had more riot than revival, but never a revival without a riot. I usually had a large bell. I would march the streets, shouting my meetings and the Gospel. Soon we had a stir in the place. We didn't know anything about diplomacy or compromise. It was all Christ or Satan. Everybody was in the camp of either one or the other. There was no *via media* as middle ground.

Many had a hard struggle before they got liberty; but once they were free, there was no scheme or devise, however unorthodox or sensational, they didn't enjoy doing. The marches through the places were strange. Sandwich boards, back and front, torches, with plenty of smoke and smell, cornets, megaphones, drums, often all going full blast at the same time.

I remember one place that was very decent, religious and dead. They said about the place that it was "pianos, pride and pious." Of course they were greatly disturbed and annoyed at me, the workers and the methods. I determined I would let them see we were just as decent as they were, so I got all the warriors to dig up their old frock suits and silk hats. You never saw such a collection – all sorts of fashions! So we put sandwich boards on them and marched through the place singing psalms. No instruments or noise.

Crowded Meetings

What a commotion! The church, hall or tent, were soon crowded, and praise God, many were well born into God's family and became our workers. We tried to make any convert, or older Christian, anything but a secret or sneak disciple. Of course, many got clean mad, but their antagonism only helped us on. They advertised us and the meetings by criticising and opposing us. I often felt very sorry for them: our strange methods and noisy parades were so upsetting to all their notions of decency and decorum.

They didn't like my preaching, at first. They said that I was coarse, vulgar, and verging on blasphemy, etc. I told them that there was one thing they couldn't deny, namely, that they could understand me. They didn't need a dictionary to do it.

I remember we came to a nice, Presbyterian, covenanting town. We had a lovely hall (a memorial to the '59 revival) seating several hundred. The first week there I never had more than maybe twenty for an audience, and mostly dear old women. The town hardly knew I was there, or was holding an evangelistic mission. I didn't know what to do. One day I met the Town Crier ringing his big bell and telling about an auction to be held. It was their way of advertising. I got an inspiration. I held out to the Crier 2s. 6d. and asked him to lend me his bell: which he did. It was a clear, starry dark night, so nice and quiet everywhere. I didn't tell anyone what I was going to do: they would have been shocked and not come with me.

I got at the top of the main street and took my coat off and tied the arms around my waist; then buckled up my sleeves and started down the street ringing the big bell and shouting with all my might, FIRE! FIRE! What a commotion! Windows were flung open, doors banged. They crowded out on the street to see me tearing down the street, roaring like a madman and ringing the bell and shouting, Fire! Fire! They thought the town was on fire. We passed the Wee Free Church. They were holding their weekly prayer meeting. They had about twelve people. Out they came, and their minister.

When I got to the bottom of the street, where there was a covenanting memorial, I climbed on it and cried out with a loud voice, "Hell fire, you covenanting Presbyterians, and I am trying to keep you out of it." I got some rubbish thrown at me, but I got my crowd and packed my hall. The minister said, any man who would do that to get people under the Gospel, he would stand by him. And he did; he came night after night to the meetings. The people said, "If he can go, then we will go too." The minister and I became fast friends, until he passed away. He was Rev. Dr. Alexander Smellie.

The Rev. J. Stuart Holden, of Portman-square Church, London, invited me to come and hold a mission in the hall connected with the church. I wondered how I would do in London. I was terribly frightened to go, but he urged me to come. He would take care of me, and help me all he could. He kept his word. What a grand band of workers he had – some titled ones among them. They had marches through the streets every night with torches, banners, and various kinds of instrument. I felt at home among them. It was a successful mission. A goodly number professed conversion.

Two strangers to me were in the meeting several nights. When we returned to the vicarage after the meeting, I met them. What a surprise. They were Dr. Wilbur Chapman and Mr. Charles Alexander. Of course, I had heard about them but never met them before. They asked me if I would like to go to America. I said I would, but only if I were sure it was God's directive will for me. They asked me to ask my committee in Scotland to give me three months' leave. They would pay all my expenses. I wasn't to preach, but attend all meetings I could and see other evangelists at work.

I was permitted to go. What an experience. I had crossed the ocean several times in a sailing vessel, but never in a luxury liner. After I had been over there three months, and seen all I could, and was about to leave, they met me and asked what I had learned. I said I thought I could preach as well as some, but I didn't know how to get results as they did. They said that was one reason why they asked me to come to America. They were soon to go to Australia with a party. They asked me would I be willing to join them and go to Australia. I consented and left the L.C.M. and home and sailed. My sphere of service was widening, and soon would become worldwide. The Lord was leading me on. Praise God!

Riot and Revival in Lanarkshire

I felt deeply and clearly that my days and work in Lanarkshire, Scotland, would soon be ended. I almost dreaded it, because I had been six years, winter and summer, holding missions there. Lanarkshire is, I suppose, the most highly populated shire in Scotland. They are mostly coal miners and steel workers. The Lord gave me great favour and affection among them. We had some wonderful missions. Many believers were led into fully yielded, Spirit-filled, soul-saving lives. And many sinners, of all kinds, were well saved, powerfully converted, and well born into God's family.

Critic Converted

During the summer we held our missions in a big tent. At one place, while erecting the tent, a big strong miner came and helped me to get the tent up. He held the pegs while I hammered them in with a 14 lb. hammer. It was sunny and hot, and I was wearing dungarees and singlet. The man said, "The way you are working would put to shame the preacher. I suppose Nicholson will come all dressed up and begin preaching after you have done all the hard work." I never let on who I was, but let him talk away about the well-fed, fat, lazy preacher. He would do no good, he said; and for his own part, he wouldn't come near a meeting! I didn't contradict him.

Our first meeting was held on the next Sunday afternoon. When I reached the platform, who should I see but my good helper. I looked at him, and he gazed at me. He evidently couldn't believe I was the man he helped put up the tent. I worked hard getting the meeting into a good happy swing, ready for the preaching. When giving the announcements and telling who I was, I said, "I have something good to tell you about the erecting of the tent." I told them about the man who helped me, and what he said about me, and added that best of all, he was here in the tent! I didn't expose him, but most of the audience knew him for a notable sinner. Maybe they didn't laugh! Best of all, he was soundly converted.

Wherever we held a mission we didn't believe in keeping quiet about it, or sitting in our tent waiting for the people to come. We believed in using many unusual means for doing this. One town we were in was a nice decent religious town. I got some dare-devil workers to put on lum hats (tall silk hats) and carry sandwich boards on their front and back. They had large printed texts of Scripture on each board. I had a fine borrowed silk hat on, a board on my back, a big drum and a large bell! Maybe we didn't create some stir and laughter!

The crowd following was great, and children noisy. We had no reputation to lose, for we had got rid of that long ago. I nearly collapsed, however, when I saw my sister coming out of the railway station with her newly-wed husband, just arriving from China. They were home on furlough, and had come to see me. They nearly collapsed, too; and poor girl, she was terribly shocked and ashamed. They turned round back to the station. Maybe I didn't hear about it.

Isn't it queer how God blessed such tactics and stirred the towns and brought crowds to attend and hear and be saved? God moves in a mysterious way His wonders to perform. He often shocks conventionality and custom, and tradition of the elders, to accomplish His purposes. He made General Joshua get his army together to conquer Jericho by marching them around the city every day for seven days. They must have seemed a silly crowd and acting ridiculously. Whoever heard of capturing a city this way. It was God's way of doing it, and it succeeded.

God's ways are not our ways. They are as high above our ways as the heavens are above the earth. God took a donkey and made it speak to Balaam, trying to keep him back from damning his own soul. Evidently Balaam understood what the donkey was saying. He was angered, and refused to do as he was told. He damned his soul by one word. He said, "If I have sinned." If he had left out the "If" and said "I have sinned," he would have been in heaven to-day, instead of being reserved unto the blackness for ever.

Old Testament Example

When Israel was being defeated by the Philistines, the Lord sent a shepherd with his sling and stone to overthrow the giant and deliver His people. Goliath, when he looked at David with his sling, said, "Am I a dog, that thou comest to me with stones?" David took the stone and slung it, and smote the Philistine in his forehead. What seeming foolishness, to bring national deliverance! God took a rooster's crowing to bring cursing, swearing, denying Peter to tears and repentance. "God hath chosen the foolish things of the world to confound the wise; and God hath chosen the weak things of the world to confound the things which are mighty: that no flesh should glory in His presence."

The early disciples turned the world upside down. They were despised and feeble, without influence, without education, without skill. Pomp, power, custom and public sentiment were all against them. They were reproached, reviled persecuted and subjected to exile and death and imprisonment. They spent years in prison, and all died there as criminals, except John, and he was exciled on Patmos among the vilest criminals. Yet within seventy years, according to the smallest estimate, there were 500,000 followers of Jesus, and some authorities affirm that there were 250,000 in the Province of Babylon alone. They increased more than 4,000-fold in sixty years. What a difference to-day we are from them.

In one of our missions I asked the workers to get a good lump of chalk and mark on the pavement from their home to the hall "Nicholson Mission" and an arrow pointing the way. They took me literally, for they whitewashed in large letters the name and arrow. The row was on by the officials for disfiguring the streets. One worker was caught and fined. He came to me and said that he couldn't pay the fine, and would have to go to jail. I encouraged him by saying that he was very fortunate, and should be proud at being jailed. He said, "How's that?" I told him he would be right in the middle of the apostolic succession. We lifted a collection and paid the fine. It was the most economical and successful advertising we did.

"Keep Moving!"

Another town would not allow open-air meetings without permission. The places we were allotted were out-of-the-way places, where few people passed by. I noticed that men selling things on the streets were not molested, as long as they kept moving. I got the workers together with their sandwich boards on them. I marched ahead of the parade ringing the bell and preaching as we marched along, but so slowly that you could hardly see us moving. What a crowd gathered along the street. The police couldn't hinder us as long as we kept moving. Our workers testified as they moved along; some gave out tracts, others distributed bills announcing our tent meetings. Many were interested; many were annoyed at us, and shouted very uncomplimentary remarks.

What prayer meetings we used to have. All nights and half nights of prayer. The noise at times was entreating and joyful. The way some prayed, you would have thought God was a million miles away, or deaf. One night when a big-voiced man was praying, one of the nice, timid, quiet prayer warriors tugged at his coat and said, "Brother, God isn't deaf." "No," said the man, "God isn't deaf, but these sinners seem to be."

One prayed, "Lord, give me a good reputation in hell and with the old devil." It created a laugh. Afterwards, I took him aside and said that he shouldn't say things at prayer to cause us to laugh. He said, "Mr. Nicholson, I didn't say it that way. I had been reading it in the Bible." I asked, "Where?" "He turned up Acts 19: 13-15, "Seven sons of Sceva..." called over the spirit possessed ones, "I adjure you by Jesus whom Paul preacheth." The evil spirit answered, and said, "*Jesus* I know, and *Paul* I know; but who are you? "He said, "I want the devil to know who I am." I couldn't say a word. He was a new convert, and had been a great sinner.

These were great days, and great victories were won. We always managed a riot or a revival. Sometimes a riot and no revival, but never a revival without a riot!

To Australia with Chapman and Alexander

The Lord has His own way of getting us ready for another move in His work and will. We do not always understand, nor can we explain the way we are to move, or when. We just have an inward feeling of assurance that we are about to move on and out, like Abram, "not knowing whither he went." I felt a wee bit annoyed and irritated, because I loved the work I was doing in Scotland, and the place and people. I had married, and had a nice wee cottage, nicely and comfortably furnished, *and paid for*. We were one in Christ Jesus, and united and agreed in the work we were doing, and the way we were doing it. Then our firstborn arrived; a daughter.

The thought of leaving all this was anything but pleasing. The Lord has a hard job on His hands with the most and the best of us. He cannot coerce or compel, but He has queer ways of making us willing until there comes a time when we are constrained to say with all our heart, "I yield; I sink by dying love compelled, and own Thee Conqueror." What rest and peace and joy fill the heart when the surrender is fully made. You begin to sing –

> *Where he may lead me I will go,*
> *For I have learned to love Him so........*
> *So onward I go, nor doubt nor fear:*
> *His divine will is sweet to me.*

Hallelujah! He gave me His promise, "Verily I say unto you, There is no man that hath left house or brethren, or sisters, or father or mother or *wife* or children or lands, for my sake, and the gospel's, but he shall receive an hundredfold now in this time, houses, and brethren, and sisters, and mothers, and children, and lands, with persecutions; and in the world to come eternal life." (Mark 10: 29-30). Notice, we will receive houses, sisters, mothers, children - all in the plural; and not in some future day but *now*. *Hallelujah*! We also get persecutions. Like salt in our food. It gives savour to our service.

I accepted, with great fear and trembling, the invitation of Dr. Wilbur Chapman and Mr. Chas. M. Alexander, to join their party, conducting evangelistic campaigns all over the world. They were beginning an Australian campaign, starting at Melbourne, Victoria, in May 1909. I was to leave London in March, and join them at Melbourne. They were going via the Pacific to Australia, while I journeyed by the Mediterranean. It was a wrench leaving wife and bairn, and the work and workers I had got to know and love. I didn't know when, if ever, I would return. But I had sure and clear leading that I was in the centre of the circle of the will of God. He would not fail me or forsake me.

I embarked at London on the S.S. *Ophir*. The vessel was crowded. I didn't know a single person aboard. Many were waving goodbye to their friends. I hadn't one to wish me goodbye. Maybe I didn't feel lonely and homesick! I had a real dose of mental malaria, ingrowing thoughts and blues. In fact, it was a good dose of old fashioned "dumps". Maybe the old devil didn't work overtime on me. He succeeded for a while in making me a pure bred unbelieving believer. The Lord is a specialist in dealing with this sort of disease. He had treated and helped Abraham, Moses, David, Jeremiah, Jonah, John Baptist etc., etc. He wonderfully helped me. Bless Him!

I had sailed several times through the Bay of Biscay in a sailing ship. But, oh, what a change now, on board a lovely big steamer, with every comfort and luxury, and all sorts of good food with no stint. On the sailing ship you had every discomfort, and the severely rationed food was neither palatable nor pleasing.

I had my deck chair and rugs, and my Bible and books; and for a time, I had very little company – so many were sea-sick. I had got over that sort of thing in my sailing ship days. I love the sea. The rising and rolling and falling of the ship was lovely. I wondered who I would meet among the passengers, and what could be done about getting sinners converted. I prayed hard for wisdom and tact, and above all, courage, and the double portion of the Spirit to enable me to please the Lord and find favour in the eyes of those I sought to save.

After a few days the weather became balmy and sunny. The decks were soon crowded. All kinds of games were played. It wasn't long before you knew many. That is one thing peculiar to travelling by steamer: you soon get to know each other very soon – all know your name, where you come from, and what your business is, and where you will be staying. To get to know all this about each other anywhere else, would take years; but on board ship all barriers soon break down. I found it fine, because I got a good chat with my inquisitive fellow travellers about their salvation. I got to know some who could say they were saved; but by many others I was shunned as if I were infected with palsy, plague and fever, and severely left alone.

I met one young man, a Navy man, and an out-and-out joyful Christian. We became close friends. We had lovely fellowship and sweet times of prayer. We found a quiet place up on deck near the life-boats, and here we chatted and prayed and met the Lord. We were not allowed to have a service on the first or second class deck. I knew also that if we asked permission to hold services on the third class deck, we should be refused. So we determined to hold services there without asking, and see if they would stop us. We held many services, right out on deck. The third class passengers were glad to see us, and sat around and sang the hymns. Many first and second class passengers stood along the rail on their deck, and listened as we sang and preached.

I believe we reached more of these two classes in this way, than if we had been allowed to hold services on their deck.

The services gave us an opening among the passengers through the day, for personal work. When we found any who were anxious or interested, we would bring them up to the boat deck where we could have quiet and privacy to deal with them.

One Thing Lacking

I remember one young fellow who was going out as an assistant minister to a big city church. He wasn't saved, and knew it; but he couldn't or wouldn't receive salvation by faith on the ground of grace. He kept saying, "It is too cheap. Too easy." He felt he would have to merit it. Of course he knew he could never wholly deserve it, but he was trying to partly deserve. It. What he lacked Christ would make it up. How many nice, decent, religious people like him there are to-day. They don't like to be under obligation to God. If God would give them some credit in their salvation, they would be saved. But to acknowledge they are undone, helpless, and totally bankrupt, is too sore on their pride, and they go away sorrowful.

What a terrible sin pride is. What a grip it has on so many. They won't accept for nothing what they will never get any other way.

> Not the labour of my hands
> Can fulfil Thy law's demands…
> All for sin could not atone;
> Thou must save, and Thou alone.

This young man never made a decision for Christ, and we never met him again.

I shall never forget the early morning we arrived at Naples. It was a Sunday. Lovely sunshine and deep blue waters – so clear that we could see the propellers fifteen feet below the water. Large parties were arranged among the passengers to visit Pompeii and see the wonderful ruins. It seemed as if my Navy friend and I were the only ones left on board. When they asked us if we were going, we said, no. They asked us why. We said it was the Lord's day, and we couldn't go joy riding on that day. They looked at us as if we were crazy. Some felt guilty and were annoyed at our attitude and testimony. But what else could we do? We had been preaching on board. We couldn't preach one thing and practise another. That would be like an old cow giving a good pail of milk and kicking it over.

Maybe it wasn't a test. We would like to have visited Pompeii's ruins. I don't think I will ever see them: it is not likely I shall be that way again. But we would have ruined our testimony if we had yielded to the old devil's temptation, and our preaching would have been in vain. The Lord made it up to us by filling our hearts with His peace and joy, and making Him so precious and real. Hallelujah!

We continued our voyage, and never had a decent storm at sea, I was disappointed. I had experienced many a good gale at sea during my time on board a sailing ship. I wondered what it would be like on a steamer. We arrived at Fremantle, West Australia; and I received word to leave the ship and take the train to Melbourne to be in time for the beginning of the campaign there. I would rather have continued the journey by boat. Being a man under authority, however, there was nothing for me to do, but obey. When I arrived at Melbourne several days after our arrival at Fremantle, I was met by some of the party. We were soon feeling at home among them. They were a fine bunch.

Campaigning in Australia and America

I arrived in Melbourne, a stranger in a strange land. I felt lonely and a wee bit homesick, and wondered how I would get on. I was only nine years converted, had only a very limited experience in evangelistic work, and was unknown. All the other members of the Chapman-Alexander party were men of long experience and world-wide fame. I had enough sense to keep silent among them, and do a lot of watching their mannerisms, methods of work, and messages. My sufficiency was in God. I wasn't dependent on myself in any way. My constant cry was –

> Oh, to be nothing, nothing;
> Only to lie at His feet.
> A broken and empty vessel, for the
> Master's use made meet.

The city was divided into sections, and all the churches in each section united in the campaign. The meetings were held in some central large hall in these sections. I was located in a large industrial area, and the venue was the town hall, Collingswood – such a lovely building, and suitable for evangelistic meetings. It seated about 2,000 and large rooms were available for dealing with enquirers.

Way to Revival

I had a singer and pianist allotted to me. We had a large choir, and a fine band of workers. Mr. Alexander thought I looked and dressed too much like a country boy, so I was fitted for a frock coat and striped trousers and a silk hat. When I was first so dressed I hardly knew myself. It nearly spoiled me, for I wondered if I would have to preach according to the dress. The Lord delivered and enabled me to forget all about how I was dressed, and seek only to please Him and lead saved ones into yielded, Spirit-filled lives, and sinners to the Saviour.

It wasn't long before we were crowded out every night. The whole district was in a turmoil. When saved ones "let go, and let God" have His way in their lives, Jesus is no longer to them as a root out of a dry ground, having no form nor comeliness, and no beauty that they should desire Him: but He becomes the Rose of Sharon, the Lily of the Valley, the bright and morning star, the fairest among ten thousand to their soul. They are spoiled for the world, its pomp and pleasures, and satisfied fully and perpetually in Him. Then the unsaved take notice of them, and come under conviction of sin and long to be saved.

This is God's way to revival. When the disciples were all filled with the Holy Ghost they began to testify by life and lip, until Jerusalem was turned upside down. The Rev. John McNeill used to say, "When it was upside down, it was right side up." Three thousand converted in one day! Another day five thousand men were converted, and soon afterwards multitudes (myriads) were added to the Church. Then the disciples were multiplied, not merely added. It was God's way that day, and it is His way to-day anywhere.

Crowded Meetings

Every night we filled the Episcopal church and the big Methodist church, as well as the town hall. They had no microphones and relay contraptions in those days, so every evening I began in the Episcopal church. My song-leader began the service and then left it to me, while he went on to begin the song service in the Methodist Church until I arrived; then on to the town hall. It didn't seem to matter what time he began the song service and I preached – and I rarely preached for less than an hour, and often longer. When you are in the midst of a Revival the clock is not considered. The Lord beats the devil every way. He can satisfy every longing. His pleasures wear well and satisfy fully.

The secular press gave little or no notice of any of the meetings anywhere. So one noon-day meeting, which Dr. Chapman held for men only every day in the Melbourne City town hall, he said it was strange that the daily papers were taking no notice of the meetings, when thousands of the people were interested in them. He suggested that it would work wonders if the businessmen would phone their papers or write to the editors, telling them that if they wouldn't take notice of the meetings they would cancel their subscription. It happened. The reporters were in every meeting of the city that very night, and throughout the mission.

When I arrived at the town hall that night, I saw a table right under the platform, and several reporters were at work. It scared me. None had been there before. However, I soon forgot all about them. The hall was crowded with people, sitting and standing everywhere. They had been there for two or more hours. The atmosphere was like pea soup, but didn't smell like soup. If I hadn't any inspiration, I had plenty of perspiration. My sermon that night was on "God's Hell." The Holy Spirit was manifestly working. I hadn't been preaching long, when some fainted and were carried out, causing great confusion because of the crowd. It didn't hinder the Holy Spirit convicting or me preaching. Many enquirers were dealt with.

The next day the leading morning papers had large headlines about the service, such as:"Appalling scenes." "Lurid evangelist." "The horrors of hell preached," etc. It created no small stir. Everywhere we went holding meetings; I was referred to as the "hell fire" preacher. You would have thought it was the only subject I preached on. Some of the party thought it was an unenviable notoriety. It didn't please me. The Lord Jesus made Himself of no reputation. As long as I had His approval and my own conscience, what need I care?

Farewell Meetings

We visited most of the large cities.   Chapman and Alexander were leaving for the Orient en route to U.S.A., to begin a simultaneous mission in Chicago. We were left behind until August, as we had to join them again at Chicago, in October, 1910. We held a whole day of meetings at Brisbane. It was our farewell. I held a meeting for ministers at 10 a.m. a businessmen's meeting at 12 noon; Bible Reading at 3 p.m.; and the final farewell meeting in the Methodist Church, 7 p.m.

We were sailing the next morning for Vancouver, B.C., and had spent a few days at Bundaberg. Our friends, the Youngs, have a large sugar plantation and sugar refinery there. They are fine out-and-out Christians, and were founders of the Solomon Island mission. We were out one day horse riding. I had a lovely Arabian horse, 17 hands high. While in the Bush a kangaroo jumped out, and we all started after it. My horse was off before I had a good hold of the reins. The bit was in his teeth. As he galloped under a large tree, I put out my right hand to save my face, and my wrist was broken. I didn't tell them it was broken, for I didn't want to bother them: I just said I thought it was a sprain.

We had to leave that night by train for Brisbane. The engine driver had been converted, and we were chatting before we left the station. He saw that my hand was swollen; and maybe it wasn't paining me. He invited me to ride on the engine and keep my hand in a bucket of cold water. I rode on the engine all night until we arrived at Brisbane early next morning. I was in time for breakfast and the ministers' meeting. One of the ministers noticed my swollen hand and asked me about it. He took me to a specialist, who put a large wooden splint over my open hand and along my arm. I couldn't get my arm into my coat sleeve, so I kept it well hidden under my coat while preaching. At the evening service, what a crowded place we had. I got warmed up during the preaching and without thinking, out went my arm, in bandage and splint, up in the air. There was a shocked surprise and a burst of laughter. The doctor took me to his private hospital for the night. He put me to sleep and eased the pain and swelling with hot packs all night. Then he took me to the steamer and put me in the care of the ship's doctor. He was a Roman Catholic doctor, and never charged me a penny.

We had a delightful passage over the Pacific, calling at Fiji and Samoa and Honolulu. I had sailed through the Pacific in a sailing ship, but this time in a luxury liner. Oh, what a change! The doctor removed the splint and found the broken wrist well healed, but a bit stiff. We left by train through Canada, and arrived in Chicago in good time and to begin the simultaneous campaign. There were seventy evangelists; each allotted a certain district, where all the churches united in a hall or church. My district was called "Little hell." They said it wasn't safe to go there without police protection, especially at night. We were never molested, and had the joy of seeing sinners converted.

A Year in Glasgow; then back to U.S.A.

The Chicago campaign came to an end. I don't think it was much of a success. It was a well organized, tremendous effort, but never seemed to make any impact on the city. There was disunity among the workers, who had been called in from all over U.S.A. and Britain. They were not all with one accord in one place. The Holy Spirit's presence and power were not manifested. The Lord does not demand unanimity, but does demand unity.

Our party left for Indiana, and while there I received a cable from Pastor D. J. Findlay, of Glasgow, asking me to take over the pastorate of the Tabernacle, as he had a breakdown in health and was going on a world tour, visiting the mission stations and missionaries he was connected with. My heart gave a jump for joy; because it would mean home and wife and child, as well as the honour and high privilege of carrying on the work while the Pastor was away. I was fearful a wee while whether it was my pleasure I was considering more than His directive will in the matter. After waiting patiently for some time, the assurance and quietness and peace filled me, as I cabled my acceptance.

St. George's Cross

Home sweet home once more. I began my ministry at the Tabernacle on January 1, 1912. What a wonderful year it was. What a wonderful crowd of willing workers there were. They took me to their heart and confidence, and gave me all they had to help, encourage and guide. I remember issuing a "pastoral letter" to the congregation, asking for their earnest, constant believing prayers on my behalf and the work of the Tabernacle. I had a perforated part of the letter, so that they could fill in their name and address and send it to me. The response was astonishing and heart cheering. It was evident that they really meant it, for every prayer meeting was attended, Sundays and Saturdays.

There wasn't a meeting of any kind that wasn't preceded by a prayer meeting. The meetings were never dry or stiff. The prayers were fervent, short and loud. When it came to all-nights and half-nights of prayer, the fire truly fell. The results at the Sunday services were heart-stirring and humbling. I don't believe we had a Sunday without many being dealt with about their soul and some well born and powerfully converted. I was told by the workers that about 900 passed through the inquiry rooms during the year. Sometimes we would have no after-meetings; but the workers were well distributed among the congregation, so that many were dealt with about their soul's salvation. An unsaved one had a hard job getting out of the service without being spoken to about salvation.

Memorable Year

Some Christians thought such work would keep sinners from coming to the services. We didn't find it to work that way. Of course some got clean mad. That was a good sign, for you never can have peace without a conflict. They have to get mad before they can become glad. And the madder they were the "gladder" when converted. The workers were really tactful, faithful and winsome.

The Tabernacle was well filled every Sunday, morning and evening, summer and winter. It seated about 1,200. The open-air meetings and marches were great. Many were *caught* this way. If ever a pastor was upheld and loved by his people, it was me. I never asked them to do anything and found them unwilling to do it, whether they saw eye to eye with it or not. We were all agreed that we were willing to be fools for Christ's sake and the salvation of the lost, for whom Christ died.

I will never forget that year at the Tabernacle. But like everything down here it came to an end. The Pastor returned to take up the work again, and I had made engagements in America beginning in January. In a way, I was glad to get away from the settled work of the pastorate and take up the work of an evangelist again. Having been roving since early days, at sea and in evangelistic work, the settled ministry had become irksome, and the spirit of wanderlust was tormenting me, at times. The Pastor and people invited me to stay with them. It was very kind of them, but I had the "itchy feet," and best of all, I had the assurance that it was His directive will for me. I don't believe it is ever God's will to put a square man in a round hole, or vice versa. He made me for an itinerant sort of life. So I feel very much at home and enjoy the journeying here and there doing God's work. To be a whole year in one place is a queer strain on my nature and the grace of God in me.

I was back in U.S.A. holding tabernacle meetings. The churches of a city would unite together and build a wooden tabernacle for the gatherings. It was neutral ground, and all churches felt free to go there. Mr. Raymond Hemmings, song leader and soloist, who was with me in Australia, assisted, as well as several other workers who joined us. The Lord graciously blessed our efforts, and we were kept busy. I was young and strong. Work was a pleasure. I felt I was lazy even to take time to sleep. I never rested between missions.

Rev. W.P. and Mrs. Nicholson with Mr. Raymond Hemmings,
Song Leader and Soloist (Centre back)

Death's Door

This didn't last. The Lord is no slave driver. I believe the old devil when he sees we are eager to work, begins to drive us on to excess, if he can't hinder us. I came to the breaking point. At the close of a campaign I collapsed and managed to get to a friend's home. The doctor was called and said I had typhoid fever, of a very malignant type. I was taken to a hospital and lay there fifteen weeks. I was delirious for three weeks, and haemorrhaged severely. When I became conscious I was only 75 lbs. weight, and so weak that I couldn't lift a hand or draw a breath. The three doctors and a specialist said I couldn't live. Prayer was made for me at many places, and the Lord answered and raised me up. Lord Maclay, of Glasgow, sent Mrs. Nicholson over to me, and brought me home. He paid all the travelling expenses. When able I went to Glasgow to preach at the Tabernacle for a Sunday. It was announced that "The man Jesus raised from the dead" would preach. I was truly and miraculously raised from the dead.

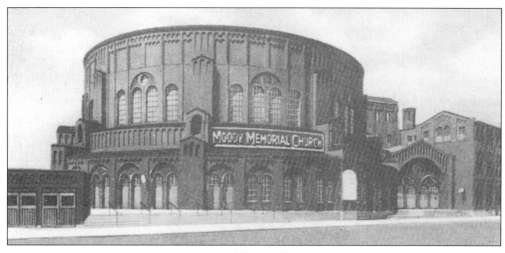

Moody Memorial Church, Chicago, Illinois.

It was a rich experience to be called by the Moody Church, Chicago, to hold a mission there. The Lord gave us a time of rich blessing to saint and sinner. We were crowded out. Overflow meetings were held in the lower auditorium. Of course the meetings were held in the old church, now demolished. While there I was entertained by the Moody Bible Institute, and occupied the bedroom of D. L. Moody and slept in his bed. Dr. James Gray was Dean of the Institute – one of God's choice gentlemen. Dr. Towner, composer of the tunes to so many of our hymns, and many others now with the Lord, were our helpers and friends.

There was one who became a very dear, loving and loyal friend, Mr. Thomas Smith. We had many a laugh over the fact that some of the audience, after a service, meeting Mr. Smith, would say, "Mr. Nicholson, we enjoyed your message to-day." We looked very much alike. I don't know whether he felt complimented or not, but I know I did. When we were in one of his apple orchards, he would walk among his trees and tell me about them, and make good application of it to our own spiritual growth and progress. For instance, he once took his knife and cut open the bark of the tree. I wondered why. He said the tree was bark-bound, so the sap could not freely flow. This hindered fruit-bearing.

Ordination to the Ministry

He had one large orchard of lovely Northern Spy apple trees. We came across several rows of trees that were unlike the others, so I said that I didn't want to contradict him, but here were trees with all their branches growing up straight, whereas most of the trees had their branches bent down. He said that these trees whose branches were straight up were young trees, and had not yet borne any fruit. When trees bear fruit the branches bent down. When we are fruit-bearing branches we are bowed down and humble. He is now with his Lord and Saviour. I have more friends in heaven than down here.

I was ordained a Presbyterian minister at Harrisburg, Penn. I don't know that it added anything to me, or the work. But it did give me a standing. They knew now I was no "wild-cat" irresponsible sort of evangelist. I came across some evangelists who, when asked what church they belonged to would say, "I belong to the Lord." I always felt a wee bit suspicious about them. I remember in one place where they wanted me for a meeting, the minister said he would have to get the permission of the Bishop. When he consulted the Bishop he said, "If he is an ordained man, it will be all right." I sent him my letter of credence, which satisfied him. He had only one condition: I was not to ask the congregation to whistle! So we held the meeting without whistling; but we had plenty of singing and shouting and laughter. Hallelujah!

Itinerating in Mid-West America

Dr. R. A. Torrey

I received one day a wire from Dr. R. A. Torrey, asking if I would occupy his pulpit in the Church of the Open Door, Los Angeles, California, during September. We were living in Carlisle, Penn. at the time. I wired accepting. We had kept this month for our summer holiday, and had rented a cottage by the sea; so the family went on holiday to the Atlantic coast, while I went to the Pacific coast to preach. My wife used to say laughingly that she "married me to get rid of me. "It looked like that sometimes!

What a fine church it was. It had two galleries around the auditorium, and seated over 4,000. You could whisper and be heard. The Bible Institute was around it – men on one side, women on the other. I was at home from the very first day. The assistant minister, Dr. T. Horton, was the keenest and most continuous soul-winner I ever met. He was a regular "hound of heaven." Every Sunday scores were led to Christ by efficient workers.

Camping Journey

When I had been there about two weeks, the Directors invited me to become the Bible Institute evangelist. I felt the Lord was leading, so consented. On my return East to bring the family out to Los Angeles, I held a mission in Dr. Riley's Church in Minneapolis, one of the largest Baptist Churches in the Mid West, with a real live soul-saving congregation.

We sold our home and chattels, and packed what we needed for the trip West, in a trailer. There were six of us – my wife and I, our three children and maid. We had a journey of 3,000 miles ahead of us. West of Chicago there was only trails, not roads. I was doing well if I managed ten miles an hour any day. It was a most interesting and enjoyable trip. We were six weeks en route, and had no mishaps along the way. The children and maid had the mumps: it helped to relieve the monotony! We camped out every night in our tent, and did all our own cooking.

We arrived in good condition, and I was soon on the war-path again. I was sent to a town which had been the centre of the '49 gold rush. There were four different churches, in which the aggregate attendance any Sunday was about thirty. The main street was filled with saloons and brothels, wide open every night and day, and well filled. My heart sank within me. The meetings were held in a dirty, ramshackle, defunct theatre. I told the ministers that we would hold an open-air meeting on the Saturday. They nearly collapsed, and said that if we did, our lives would be in danger. I replied, "Brethren, blessed are the dead that die in the Lord."

Riotous Open-Air Meeting

We went to the middle of the town and the middle of the street. The only musical weapon we had was a sort of fiddle belonging to the Methodist minister. I said that I would raise the tune, and if he could follow me on the contraption, to make as much noise as he could. I had a good voice. The ministers had never needed to raise their voices in their wee churches; and as for speaking at an open-air meeting, it was "infra dig."

We had hardly begun singing when the doors were banging open, and out the drunken crowd came. They were speechless for a wee while, astounded. My heart was beating like a lamb's tail when drinking its mother's milk. I glanced at the preachers, who looked as if they would faint any minute. Their singing was only a whisper. But I kept roaring away. Then I told the crowd that we were a bunch of ministers of the town, and that we would be holding revival meetings every night in the theatre.

By this time they were yelling at me and at each other. I saw there was no chance of being heard preaching, so I up and at them and told them that Americans believed in free speech and free assembly. I said "A lot of you fellows believe this; but some of those who are kicking up a row are not Americans and will you allow them to hinder our meeting?"

This got them fighting among themselves. They didn't know who they were fighting, or why they were fighting, or what they were fighting for. I turned to the preachers and said, "Skip quietly out and away home." I slipped out of the crowd and into my hotel, where I stood and looked at the crowd fighting, some for me and some against. It was a real Donneybrook Fair fight. I was getting the best widespread publicity of my meetings!

On the Sunday afternoon I got the ministers to come with me and hold several open-air meetings in the decent part of the town. They stuck by fine. The old theatre was crammed, and praise God, some respectable and out-and-out sinners were saved. They both needed saving, the one as much as the other.

I said to the ministers one day, "We ought to have a day of fasting and praying." They had never heard of such a thing. They thought it wasn't necessary, because we had the crowd and some conversions. But they gave in to me. I piled them into my car early one morning, and we made for a hill outside the town, called Jackass Hill. We were there some time making nice quiet prayers, that wouldn't disturb the devil or do violence to the kingdom of Heaven. Around about noon the breaking, melting, moulding, filling began. Then praying really began with strong cries and tears.

I heard a rustling in the bushes, and looked to see who was there. Several miners, with their wee lamps on their caps, were standing with their mouths and eyes wide open. They couldn't understand it. I said "Men, we are gathered as ministers, praying for you. We are concerned about you going to hell so unconcerned, and we are trying to get you saved." At this they took to their heels, and spread abroad what they had seen and heard. All this was advertising the meetings and creating conviction abroad.

Towns like this rarely have a mission or hear the Gospel. I remember another town in which we held a mission. It was located near a large copper mine. The meetings were at first held in a nice wee respectable Presbyterian church, holding about 200, but away from the centre of the town. There were just a handful of people attending the services, and making no increase or result. I saw the main street every night crowded with miners. There were saloons, galore, wide open and well filled; and here we were with our decent wee church and handful of people.

I did not consult anyone, because I felt they would never agree; but I found a good-sized dancing hall to let, above a saloon. I hired it cheap, but had to pay in advance – I suppose they thought it wouldn't be long before I was run out of the town! You would have laughed to see the faces of my wee bunch and their minister when I told them that the meetings were to be held in the hall the next Sunday and every night after. You could have knocked them down with a straw, or heard their hearts beat. I confess that I wasn't far behind them in their feelings, but I was sure we were leading in His will.

The hall was crowded. What a motley crowd! I had a hard job of getting them quieted. I threatened that I would throw them down the stairs if they wouldn't behave. It was all bluff. Maybe I would have been in a fix if even one had dared me to throw him out. Nine-tenths of courage is bluff.

I suddenly had an attack, just before meeting time. I thought I was going to die. The only doctor in the town was hundreds of miles away on a case. The local nurse gave me a shot that eased the pain. I had a job preaching, and was awfully weak. The doctor came and examined me, but couldn't be sure what it was, but he thought it was appendicitis. He said I ought to cancel the meetings, make for Los Angeles, and be examined. I said that I couldn't do that; I would finish the mission on Sunday. I had Friday, Saturday and three services on Sunday. The Lord surely helped me, and what a fine number of men and others came out for Christ.

I arrived home and was examined by three doctors. They were not sure what was wrong but certainly something serious; so they decided on an explorative operation. I was put in the hospital to be operated on next morning. It is a queer feeling you have when waiting for the operation. An unknown lady wrote me a letter giving me Proverbs 3: 24, "When thou liest down, thou shalt not be afraid: yea, thou shalt lie down, and thy sleep shall be sweet." Hallelujah! It was a bad appendix.

The Lord has His own ways about guiding us and making us willing to do His will. My father had passed away at 90. I got a longing to go back to Bangor and see my dear old mother. I thought this would be a good time, and that I could recuperate after the operation. The Directors were agreeable, but made me promise that I would come back – which I did. I don't believe I could have got away home, had I not been ill, for there was so much work ahead. But my operation made me ready and willing to go.

Civil War and Revival in Ulster;
Keswick and Cambridge

When we arrived in Ulster we found the country terribly disturbed. Soon there was civil war. Much property was burned; many lives were lost. Feelings were on fire. Curfew was enforced, and the city of Belfast was a deserted place; but all public lights were in full blaze. I remember one night standing on the Queen's Bridge and looking back over the city. It looked like a doomed city. There were some dozen or more large fires all over the city. My eyes were dim with tears.

In the midst of all this we began our first mission in the city. It was held in the Albert Hall, Shankhill Road. Dr. Henry Montgomery was the founder and minister of the mission. It is one of the largest auditoriums in Belfast. Those coming to the meetings had to lie flat in the tram cars, because bombs were thrown at the cars as they passed by. During the meetings we could hear shots being fired. In spite of all this, the hall was crowded out night by night, and hundreds turned away. Best of all, many were deciding for Christ at every service, mostly men, and nearly all of them ship yard workers.

Memorable Experiences

You could tell there was a revival there; not one worked up, but prayed and worked down. The times were such. It was man's extremity, but, glory to God! God's opportunity.

We had no choir or soloist. I was always scared of a choir. They are usually the devil's war office. The congregation was the choir. And believe it or not, I was the song leader as well as preacher. I couldn't tell one note from another. When I looked at a music book, the wee black notes seemed to me like starlings on telegraph wires. I knew some tunes, but we used many keys in every hymn. We never used a big organ: they were too unwieldy. We had a piano or wee organ, but often never an instrument. I always told the pianist, if there was one, not to raise or begin the hymn tune, but to leave that to me. I could hold a tune, but what key bothered me. We always got started, however, and they all followed. It was laughable to see the poor pianist with his ear close to the piano trying to find the key.

We would sing one hymn or psalm over and over again, and without a stop change over to another hymn or chorus. Those soured and cynical, or critical and opposed, were not long in this kind of atmosphere until they were smiling and singing. You cannot have spring time without singing birds and flowers; and you can't have a revival without singing.

This would last for an hour or so. Then the reading of the Bible, and an exposition. Then a text and sermon lasting usually an hour or more. The place crowded out, and standing in the aisles and window sills, side rooms and pulpit stairs! Never a move until all was over. When God gives a revival you forget all about time.

I didn't keep them singing and having a good time, and merely making them happy. Oh no. I was getting them ready for the preaching. Their prejudices and worries were all cleared up. You can't get a revival in a stiff, starchy congregation or church.

One night the Island men (ship yard workers) came in a procession, hundreds strong headed by the vicar. They were in their dungarees and dirt. They did not go home for their dinner. The women met them and gave them something to eat as they marched and shouted. The church railings were torn up and carried away, as they charged for the doors. Soon the place was crammed like sardines in a tin. They made a collection to put up new railings before the church, and put a tablet on them which said, "In memory of the night of the Big Push, when 259 men decided for Christ." All glory and power be His forever and ever.

The 'Island men' (ship yard workers) who attended the meetings in their thousands
Photograph Courtesy of Harland & Wolff

Shock for the Sedate

Some very nice church-going people were shocked, and were much opposed, because of the happy informality of the meetings. They didn't see that more than half of the congregation were anything but church people. The Lord was using the means to bring the non-church crowd into the church. The ministers and workers of the church could straighten them out, teach them after the mission was over. We were in the quarry, blasting out the stones. Of course there is noise, dust and confusion. The stones after being quarried are cut and smoothed and fit for the building. We mustn't confuse the quarrying and the preparing. I would stand on my head in the pulpit if it would help win a man for Christ.

At one of the missions in a fine church, the minister asked me to behave myself and control the congregation, and stop whistling and shouting, and especially to modify my language; to try to preach the love of God, and not hell and damnation, etc. He said that he felt sick in the service the night before, my message was awful. I replied, "It is a pity you didn't wait and see over 200 come out for Christ, mostly men." He asked if I would not preach on the love and mercy of God. I said, "I will change my message tonight, and see the result." I preached my heart out. Tears were on many faces. But only about twelve decided for Christ. He said it was a great sermon. "Yes," I said, "you are more concerned about sermons than about souls. I am out for souls."

There was every evidence that it was God's revival. Hatreds were healed; shooting was gone, and there was shouting for joy. Debts long standing were being paid.

Restitution was on every hand. Stolen tools and goods were returned. Grudges and bitternesses were wiped out. Church members were increased. Prayer meetings were revived. Sunday School scholars multiplied. Open air meetings were to be seen at many street corners, where shouting and fighting had taken place – the meetings held by those who formerly were the rioters. Truly the Lord was in our midst, and our mouth was filled with laughter, and there was much joy in the presence of God over sinners repenting.

Culminating Campaign

We held some twelve or thirteen missions in Belfast alone. Every mission was for four weeks and five Sundays. Some of our "friends" said that the revival was petering out, and I was a spent force. The last mission was held in August, in the Assembly Building – the most beautiful and largest hall in the city. Many members of the hall committee were opposed to letting it for the mission. They said the hall would be wrecked; but some of them said, "Let us give them the hall during August, the summer holiday month. We will all be out of the city and the mission will be a wash out." They thought I would be discredited and have to leave the country.

The meetings were crowded out every night. The 8 p.m. service usually began around 7 p.m. Best of all, hundreds decided for Christ; and there wasn't a chair damaged, or a scratch on the walls. The rent of the hall was paid one week before the close of the mission. Praise God! Unto Him be all the glory.

The missions held in the large towns throughout Ulster were one succession of real revivals. Who could ever forget Ballymena mission? The church services began shortly after 6 p.m. instead of 8 p.m. This didn't mean that they ended any earlier! Every place in the church was crowded, even the window sills. Every now and then during the service there was the noise of a broken pane of glass. It took about £70 to fix the windows of the church after the mission. There were more conversions in this mission than any other.

We had six weeks at Londonderry, "the maiden city," for it is said that "It is often wooed but never won." Hundreds were won during the mission. The results of that mission have been remarkably lasting. A Christian Workers Union was formed, to conserve the results and carry on the work. The Union has carried on the work through the years. They have the largest hall for the Sunday after-church services, where large numbers gather, and souls are saved every service since the mission – mostly among young men and women.

I was invited by the Keswick Convention Council to conduct the two Sunday evening evangelistic services of the Convention Week. It was grand to see scores come forward seeking Christ as Saviour. They had been seeking the second blessing and had not received the first. We held the open air meetings during the week. What crowds, and thank God, good results.

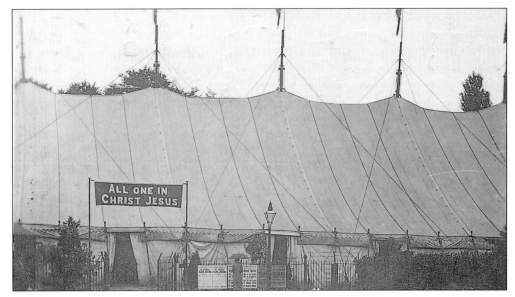

Keswick Convention Tent

The service is over and the congregation exit the Tent
Note the number of children present

Dr. Stuart Holden asked me to come to Cambridge to meet the personal workers, in view of the Triennial Mission to be held there. When I arrived at London, I met some of the C.I.C.C.U. members. They said that Dr. Holden had had a stroke, and would not be able to conduct the mission. There was only one thing they could do, and that was asked me to take his place. I nearly collapsed. I knew my limitations, and that it was presumptuous on my part to take the mission. I was persuaded: and what a time we had! What crowds of men, and what blessed results. The students couldn't have treated me better. I did enjoy it.

Farewell

My reminiscences have come to an end. If my experiences have been any encouragement or help to any, I have been well rewarded. I hope all have marvelled and wondered at the grace of God that could stoop so low and lift so little, and use me in His service. Truly it is said, "Not many wise men after the flesh are called. But God hath chosen the foolish, the weak, the base, the despised, the nothings, that no flesh should glory in His presence." The world has yet to see what God can do for, and with, a man providing he won't touch the glory.

I am now on the retired list, and nearing the end of the road. I have had a long and good innings. A sinner saved, and sanctified by grace, and kept safe by the power of God through faith unto salvation.

> My Lord, how full of sweet content,
> I pass my years of banishment:
> Where'er I dwell, I dwell with Thee,
> In heaven, in earth, or on the sea.
> To me remains nor place, nor time;
> My country is in every clime:
> I can be calm, and free from care,
> On any shore, since God is there:
> While place we seek or place we shun,
> The soul finds happiness in none:
> But with God to guide our way,
> 'Tis equal joy to go or stay.
> -Guyon.

"I am now ready, and the time of my departure is at hand. I have fought a good fight, I have finished my course, I have kept the faith: henceforth there is laid up for me a crown of righteousness, which the Lord shall give me at that day: and not to me only, but unto all them also that love His appearing." (2 Timothy 4: 6-8). Maranatha. Hallelujah!

The

Nicholson

Family

Album

A Nicholson family gathering
W.P. is second from the left

Some of the older generation of the Nicholson family
W.P.s mother is seated left

W. P. Nicholson with his wife and three children

The three Nicholson
William Patteson, James and Louis

Cotton House, near Bangor
The Nicholson family home

The yard and outhouses of Cotton House with family members

PART II

NEWS, VIEWS, IMPRESSIONS

& PERSONAL LETTERS

COVERING THE MINISTRY OF

REV. W. P. NICHOLSON

1913

County Down Spectator – 22nd August 1913

A POPULAR BANGOR EVANGELIST

Mr. W. P. Nicholson's Work
An Interesting Study

As most of our readers are probably aware the hero of this article is at present in Bangor, recuperating after the serious attack of pneumonia to which he nearly succumbed while engaged in evangelical work in America.

We owe all the following from the "Southern Cross," published in Australia:-

A few years ago, when Mr. Alexander was in the midst of a Mission in England, he came across a young man who was making his mark as an evangelist. He was about thirty years of age, not tall, but powerfully built, and with a volume of love for the service of God in his heart that shone in his eyes and rang in his strong North of Ireland voice. Mr. Alexander enlisted his services, tested his work, and was so deeply impressed that before he left America he cabled to him to meet him in Australia. It was Mr. W. P. Nicholson, and he came. Mr. Alexander told the committee about him, and they decided that he was just the man for Collingswood, or the biggest Sydney crowd. So to Collingswood and Leichhardt they sent him, with Mr. J. Raymond Hemminger – and Collingswood and Sydney will never cease to thank God for that fact.

A Thumbnail Portrait

Mr. Nicholson is strongly reminiscent of the Scottish John McNeill – a son of the people, a man of robust frame and striking personality, a speaker of great plainness of speech, relieved by the saving gift of humour. As he stands on the platform to deliver the message of God, he presents a striking picture, and from the opening sentence to the closing appeal, the people are held enchained by the magnetism of his personality –a personality shot through and through with the Spirit of God. Mr. Nicholson is the unique man of the party. The Americans have much in common. Mr. Nicholson stands alone in personal appearance, in accent, and even in methods. But he preaches the same precious Gospel, and like his great colleague Dr. Chapman, he gets the crowds very largely because he knows men, especially the men of the street. He grips this class because he talks the language of the masses, and not the technical and theological language of the schools; moreover, a crowd appreciates a hard hitter. If, as one writer has described him, Mr. Alexander is the anaesthetist of the party, Mr. Nicholson is the surgeon; he believes in the use of the scalpel. But he wounds to heal. The chief secret, however, of his success is his evident consecration. It was a tradition of ancient Thebes that from the hour of his consecration the Archon never allowed the consecrates spear to pass out of his hand. All through his evangelistic career Mr. Nicholson has held the consecrated spear, and has wielded it with great power, but never with greater power than at Collingswood.

A Romantic Career

His history reads like a modern chapter of the Acts of the Apostles. He was born at Bangor, in the North of Ireland, thirty-six years ago, and was educated at Belfast. At the age of seventeen he was an apprentice on a sailing-vessel, and in this capacity he visited Australia, touching at Adelaide. Crossing over to Africa, he left the vessel at Capetown and laboured on the construction works of the Cape-to-Cairo Railway. During this time he led a wicked life, and was greatly addicted to drink. Tired of the life he was living, he returned to Bangor, and a fortnight later the power of God came down upon him in a miraculous way, and, alone in his mother's home, there came to him the experience of personal salvation.

A Changed Life

Mr. Nicholson's conversion in the way indicated shatters the "Argus" theory of conversion by hypnotic suggestion. According to another press writer, this great change in his life must be attributed to psychical phenomena. He calls it a new birth, and believes it to be the work of the Holy Spirit.

After spending a year in Belfast in business, he left for Glasgow, and entered the Bible Training Institute for two sessions. Later, he laboured as an evangelist under the Lanarkshire Christian Union, and continued in this work for five years, holding missions in the southern parts of Scotland, and later in the historic Portman Square Church, London, on the invitation of the vicar, the Rev. Stuart Holden. Mr. Alexander first heard of Mr. Nicholson through Mr. Holden, who strongly recommended him as an evangelist of great power, and after hearing him preach, and noticing his successful methods of dealing with seekers in the after-meeting, Mr. Alexander invited him to go over to America for three months, where he conducted missions in Philadelphia, New York, and Collingswood, New Jersey.

Returning to Scotland, he completed his term with the Lanarkshire Union, and then definitely joined forces with Mr. Alexander. Under his direction, Mr. Nicholson held successful missions in Glasgow, and London, and other English centres. Before leaving America on his present tour, Mr. Alexander cabled inviting him to engage in mission work in Australia, because in his own words, "I know the man and his secret of dealing with men, and believe he will be made a great power in Australia."

5th August 1919 – Bangor as it was just prior to Rev. Nicholson's ministry in Northern Ireland, showing the Pickie area with Lenaghan's Boats on the right and the Christian Workers stand almost directly above it

Courtesy of Bangor Heritage Centre

1920

From: W. P. Nicholson 'Flame for God in Ulster' by S.W. Murray

MISSIONS
BANGOR – October 1920

The mission in Bangor was held in October 1920, following widespread and intense prayer preparation. Dozens of prayer meetings were held in the preceding weeks, mostly in private homes. To quote a contemporary account:

"Though a prophet in his own country and to his own people, the reception he (Mr. Nicholson) got was marvellous. The crowds attending the services overflowed the large hall, and sinners of every kind were attracted, many of whom being won for Christ. A great work of grace was accomplished, and the society, which had so nobly stood in the breach for years and fought a good fight, was quite transformed. Larger buildings had to be procured to accommodate the converts, as well as to provide for the growth of the work. As a result of the mission too, Christian Endeavour and other meetings were started, and the whole religious life of the town was revived."

Invitations came from other centres, but Mr. Nicholson was unable to accept any commitments for some months owing to the series of missions in Scotland. This lapse of time, however, enabled a more thorough preparation to be made for future missions than had been possible in Bangor.

W.P. Nicholson John 3. 30 'Pray for me'

1921

PORTADOWN – May 1921

In May 1921 he commenced a united mission in Portadown with wide support from the churches and leaders of the community. The mission began in circumstances which might well have discouraged the organisers – the great coal strike had started and a dock strike prevented the evangelist crossing from Glasgow to begin on the advertised day, so there had to be a week's delay in the opening of the mission. During the first two weeks the First Presbyterian Church was packed out and this also happened for the concluding half in Thomas Street Methodist Church. A report of the mission stated:

"Mr. Nicholson gained the ear of the people in a marked degree and although uncompromising in his condemnation of smoking and dancing and the picture show, and presenting the bald alternatives of "Christ or Hell," even those who disagreed with him came under his spell and were converted. Over 900 names were registered as of those accepting Christ and whole families became one in Him."

Another report speaks of many of the converts being

"notable brands plucked from the burning and they make no secret of their changed lives."

One lasting effect of the mission was to be seen in the Christian Endeavour Movement. The few societies connected with local churches were doubled in membership, and in one case trebled. In addition six new societies were formed as a result of the mission. A Christian Worker's Union was formed on the lines of the Bangor one and began a vigorous evangelistic work.

LURGAN – September 1921

The following September, a similar mission was held in the neighbouring town of Lurgan. Here too there was a manifest spirit of unity and deep concern for the condition of both church and state. The services were in the High Street Presbyterian Church and one report speaks of the town having had a "tremendous upheaval" through the mission. The number of professed decisions for Jesus Christ was similar to Portadown and the effects on both church life and the outsider were startling.

NEWTOWNARDS – November 1921

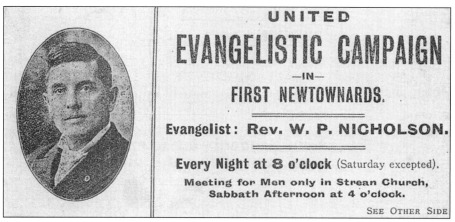

The Newtownards United Mission followed in November. The services were held in the large First Presbyterian Church and here also similar scenes took place. One elderly man who had recollections of the 1859 Revival said that some of the effects of the Holy Spirit's working even exceeded what happened in '59. A local minister reported:

"It is a sufficient testimony to the widespread feeling which prevails in the town to say that ministers are being stopped in the street by people who are anxious about their relationship with God, and that daily the homes of Christian workers are being sought out by old and young, that they may learn the way of life. The outstanding feature is the number of men in mid-life who have stood and confessed openly their willingness to accept Christ. Never in his wide and varied experience has the evangelist seen such a marked and definite movement amongst men bordering on or over fifty years of age. This in itself is a testimony to the stability and strength, and depth, and thoroughly masculine character of the work being done. Often a supercilious and short sighted judgement wags its head and says regarding evangelistic work, "It is the usual turn for old women and children." Nobody can say that of the movement in our town. The work began amongst the men and is largely carried out by men.

A sequel to the Newtownards campaign occurred two months later in connection with a mission conducted by the two ministers of the circuit in University Road Methodist Church, Belfast, during which it was reported that over a hundred professed decisions for Christ were registered. Among these were many boys and girls from a neighbouring grammar school. A report in the Irish Christian Advocate refers to one particular meeting –that of the concluding Friday, described as a most stirring occasion:

"Four young men from Newtownards, who were converted at Mr. Nicholson's mission voluntarily came and gave their experience. A profound impression was made and many cards were signed."

1922

LISBURN – January 1922

Another mission followed in Lisburn with profound effect on the churches and the community generally.

The Lisburn Standard – 6 January 1922
UNITED PROTESTANT MISSION

Mr. Nicholson strikes Right Note on Arrival
Opinions May Differ as to Methods but Not as Regards Essentials
Great Crowds Flock to Hear Outspoken Evangelist
Hardened Gambler's conversion

The eagerly anticipated mission, which the Protestant Churches of Lisburn have united in inviting Rev. W. P. Nicholson, of Los Angeles, to conduct, was commenced at the weekend. On Saturday evening, the ministers of the various churches and representative Christian workers met in the Temperance Institute to welcome the Missioner.

Rev. Canon Carmody, M.A., who was the first speaker, referred to the success which had followed Mr. Nicholson's efforts in Portadown, Lurgan, and elsewhere, and expressed the belief that similar success would result in Lisburn since they were depending upon the power of the Holy Spirit and were resolved to give the Missioner all the help in their power.

Rev. Mr. Nicholson, in his reply, expressed the pleasure it gave him to visit Lisburn as the helper of the churches in their united effort to win men for Christ and the Church. If after the mission, the Churches were not stronger in numbers, purer in spirit, mightier in faith, then he (Mr. Nicholson) would consider the mission to have been a failure. For success, it was necessary that they should pull heartily together. Opinions might differ as to the methods adopted, even to some particular form of the message, but these things were only secondary; let them put the emphasis on the first things and give their best during the campaign.

Rev. R. W. Hamilton, M.A., in his welcome, emphasised how deeply the sincerity and sanity of Mr. Nicholson had impressed him.

Rev. R. H. S. Cooper, J. N. Spence, J. J. C. Breakey, T. G. Keery, Captain Robb (Salvation Army), and Mr. Arthur Pim also joined in the welcome.

Later in the evening a meeting of the mission workers was held in the Boys' Hall, Rev. R. W. Hamilton, M.A., presiding.

Mr. Nicholson gave a short but characteristically stimulating and practical address. After this meeting the workers formed up in procession and, led by the Lisburn Temperance Silver Band, visited the different parts of the town in order to announce the mission.

The Watch-Night Service in the Methodist Church on Saturday night and the New Year's morning service in Railway Street Presbyterian Church were both conducted by Mr. Nicholson.

Orange Hall Crowded

Lisburn Orange Hall where the Mission Commenced

For the first of the mission services, the Orange Hall was crowded on Sunday afternoon. After the opening exercises, in which Rev. Canon Carmody led in prayer, Mr. Nicholson, in an earnest and reasoned address, set forth what he termed the "planks" in his platform on the basis of which he invited the co-operation of all those who followed Christianity, and sought the extension of God's Kingdom. These "planks" were – Belief in God; in the deity of Jesus Christ; in the deity and personality of the Holy Spirit; in the Bible as the Word of God; in Heaven and in hell; in the total Depravity of man; in the universality of salvation through the Holy Spirit. The address, which was listened to with earnest attention, closed with an impassioned appeal to professing Christians to seek the fitness for and then to throw themselves into the service of Christ.

At night it was found impossible to accommodate all those who wished to be present at the service, the Orange Hall being crowded before the advertised house. Mr. Nicholson took as the subject of his address "John the Baptist," and in a pictorial and strikingly impressive manner the salient features of the Baptist's character were set forth and applied to the life of the modern Christian. The appeal of the address was emphasised by the evident sincerity of the speaker, and deeply stirred those present.

Growing Intensity of Feeling

Large crowds have filled the Orange Hall at the services during the week, and a growing intensity of feeling and deepening interest have been evident as the days passed. Night by night Mr. Nicholson has dealt with the obligations and privileges of the Christian life in a way that has brought conviction to the heart and conscience and created the desire for a higher and more abundant life on the part of many who have been present at the services.

On Monday evening a large contingent of converts of the Newtownards Mission was present at the service, and those who had the opportunity of hearing the testimony of a leading business man of that town, who had been a confirmed gambler, are not likely to forget the story. At this service Mr. Nicholson spoke on "How to run a Church!"

The careful preparation preceding the mission is already being felt. Although no direct appeal has yet been made, the hearts of those responsible for the effort have been gladdened by the tidings of men and women already seeking and finding Christianity.

The Lisburn Standard – 13th January 1922

The Nicholson mission continues to excite an ever widening interest both friendly and critical. At all the services of the present week many have had to turn away unable to obtain admission. Mr. Nicholson for the present continues his addresses to Christians on the work of the Holy Spirit, and striking testimonies have been received that they are being blessed to many.

Owing to previous arrangements the services of Wednesday and Thursday evenings could not be held in the Orange Hall, but through the courtesy of the minister and Committee, the Railway Street Presbyterian Church was made available not only for these services, but for the remainder of the mission, a kindness which the mission committee greatly appreciate. There is no doubt that the Church is a more suitable building for such services; in addition to the extra seating capacity, estimated to be at least 25 per cent more, the suite of rooms available as enquiry rooms will prove of inestimable value as the mission progresses.

One feature of the services has been the numbers of men attending, and arrangements have been made to reserve the entire gallery for men in the future.

The missioner's methods have come in for much criticism, but those in closest touch with the work recognise the sanity that underlies all that is done. The very strangeness and unorthodox character of these things have proved an irresistible attraction as the multitudes who desire to be present at the meetings conclusively prove. It may seem, to those who have never heard it, a most irreverent proceeding to make the congregation whistle in a religious service, but we assure our readers it is far from being so, whilst from the practical side of quietly learning new tunes it is of the greatest value.

The greatest amount of adverse criticism comes from those who have not been present at the meetings, much of it malicious falsehood. However, to borrow one of Mr. Nicholson's phrases, "Half of the lies we hear are not true, you would be a fool to believe the other half." The one thing that cannot be gainsaid is that the hearts of men and women are being stirred with the desire for higher things.

We strongly advise any critics amongst our readers to hear Mr. Nicholson, not once or twice, but till the strangeness of the method is forgotten and we venture to predict that the spirit of criticism will soon die.

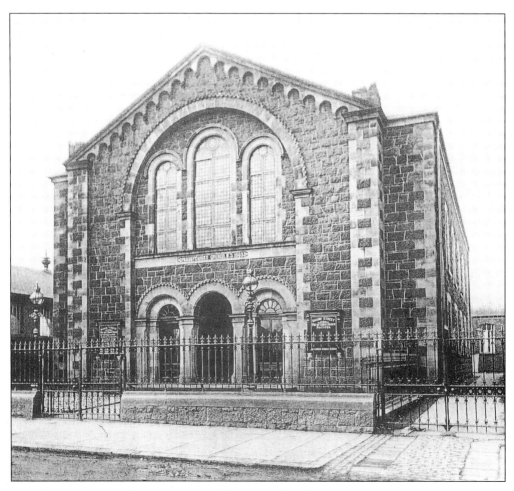

Railway Street Presbyterian Church, Lisburn c.1914

The Lisburn Standard – 20th January 1922

Interest in the United Mission now being conducted by Rev. W. P. Nicholson continues to grow; night after night the spacious Railway Street Church is packed to its utmost capacity with an audience often double the nominal seating capacity of the building, many being content with standing room, and even then almost every night folk have to turn away unable to obtain admission. Coigns of vantage outside the building have been sought by adventurous spirits eager to hear Mr. Nicholson's fitly and powerful messages.

Amongst the special features of the services held during the week have been the daily prayer meeting in the Boys Hall, at 3.30; the large numbers of men always present, more than three-fourths of the entire gallery being reserved for them; the irresistible spirit of conviction which has rested upon the gathering night after night, more than four hundred persons having passed through the Enquiry Room since Sunday night.

On Monday night when Mr. Nicholson preached under the auspices of the local branch of the White Ribboners on "The Public-House – A human Slaughter House" – almost 1,800 thronged the Church and listened with strained attention to one of the most terrible indictments of the drink traffic ever heard in Lisburn.

(Poem quoted by Rev. W. P. Nicholson in the above mentioned sermon)

"THE BAR"

A bar to heaven and a door to hell;
Whoever named it, named it well;
A bar to manliness and wealth,
A door to want and broken health;
A bar to honour, pride and fame,
A door to sin and grief and shame;
A bar to hope, a bar to prayer,
A door to darkness and despair;
A bar to honoured, useful life,
A door to brawling, senseless strife;
A bar to all that is true and brave,
A door to every drunkard's grave;
A bar to joy that home imparts,
A door to tears and aching hearts;
A bar to heaven, a door to hell
Whoever named it named it well.

The Lisburn Standard – 27th January 1922

The services have steadily grown in power of appeal, and each night scores have responded to the Missioner's appeal. More than 800 persons have passed through the enquiry room during the past ten days.

On Wednesday, Mr. Nicholson began a series of quiet hour services, which were held each afternoon at 3 o'clock, and at these services also the spacious building was filled.

The mission will enter upon its last week on Sunday, when Mr. Nicholson will preach three times in Railway Street Church. At 2 p.m. there will be a special service for women, when Mr. Nicholson will speak on "Popular Amusements - Dancing, Cards etc." At 4 p.m. the meeting will be for men only, the subject being "The Devil's Bargain" and 8 p.m. there will be the usual evangelistic service.

One of the most powerful and effective addresses yet delivered by Mr. Nicholson was that which he preached on Sunday night last on "The Unpardonable Sin." No address of the series has caused more comment or produced such an impression.

Railway Street, Lisburn - 1963
Much as it looked during the Nicholson era.

The following Chorus was known as Rev. W. P. Nicholson's doxology and was sung at the end of many meetings.

DOWN IN THE DUMPS
(Music and Words)

The Lisburn Standard – 3rd February 1922

COUNSEL TO CONVERTS
(by Rev. W. P. Nicholson)

Dear Friend,

It has given me great joy to hear you confess your desire and determination to accept Christ as your Saviour and follow Him by faith and faithfulness daily.

Nothing would give me greater grief than to hear you had not carried out your determination, but had gone back to the beggarly elements of the world again. I am sure you desire to walk worthy of the Lord unto all pleasing, being fruitful in every good work and increasing in the knowledge of the Lord. If this desire is to be gratified you must attend to the following essentials:

FIRST- Be baptised (if not baptized already) and unite with the church of your choice at the earliest opportunity.

SECOND – Be regular in your attendance upon all services of the church, especially the mid-week prayer meeting, and never fail to take part.

THIRD – Be a proportionate and a systematic giver of your income to Christ's cause and work for Christ in the church, especially trying to win others to the Lord Jesus and the church.

FOURTH – Be sure and take time daily to read the Bible and pray. The best time for this is the first thing every morning. If you are the head of the home, erect the FAMILY ALTAR and at least once a day gather the family together for prayer. Be careful about this as it is necessary to your Christian life. Be sure to join the Pocket Testament League.

FIFTH – Be sure and immediately confess your sins and if you fail or stumble don't be discouraged, but ask the Lord to forgive you. The moment you confess your sins you are forgiven whether you feel it or not. HE said it, and you believe it. Then claim the promised Holy Spirit to fill you so that you may have victory and power in the future. Do not trust your own strength or your own resolutions, they are only as strong as yourself, but trust the Lord. He never fails. REMEMBER, you can never trust yourself too little or the LORD too much.

"Nicholsonians"

Have you noticed how many promises are made in the Bible to those who live the overcoming life?

* * *

There are three classes of people in the world. There are those who exist; there are those who live; there are those who reign, but the vast bulk of the people are people who merely exist.

* * *

The Church member who professes Christianity and signs for a liquor license, is so low down that he 'has to reach up to touch bottom'.

* * *

> They may say the devil has never lived,
> They may say the devil has gone,
> But simple folks would like to know
> Who carries his business on!

* * *

God has given us two wings – faith and prayer – but the sad thing is so many have allowed Satan to clip them.

* * *

It doesn't do any good to sit up against a hot air hole and sing 'Rescue the Perishing'.

* * *

When God said "Put off the old man," he didn't say, "Put on the old woman". He said "Put on the new man."

* * *

If I were a Sherlock Holmes, and ate and slept with some of you, I wouldn't be able to find a trace of Christianity.

* * *

The religion of some is like a coat that you put on on Sunday and discard the rest of the week.

* * *

We can never swing Lisburn to God unless we roll up our sleeves and work and sweat.

* * *

You parents teach your children to dance and to play cards and what not. Do you ever teach them to pray?

* * *

The worldly man has no pleasures, except those he is ashamed of, that the Christian does not enjoy.

* * *

The devil is a clever angler; he covers the hook with the very kind of bait the fish like.

The Lisburn Standard – 3rd February 1922
(Each week the local paper carried an entire sermon preached at the Mission)
Another Record Sale

Last week we mentioned that the sale of the "Standard" the previous Friday had broken all records. Last Friday itself beat that again by a very long way. To-day, we are able to announce in advance, that last week's sale has been left far behind long before the paper has gone to press at all. Thousands of copies, over and above our ordinary circulation, have been booked, and orders are still tumbling in from all over the country. Certainly we have to thank Mr. Nicholson for introducing the "Standard" into many distant homes where, we dare say, they never even knew there was such a paper. We hope to give another of Mr. Nicholson's addresses in our next issue.

Evidence (of Mission Influence)

There was only one case for hearing at Lisburn Petty Sessions yesterday – a charge of simple drunkenness against a small farmer who resides some miles outside Lisburn; and there was not a single case listed for the Town Court. This is a unique happening and will no doubt be attributed – and rightly we think – to the Mission. For weeks past now the Court has been regarded by the unemployed and habitual loafer as a sort of free entertainment. Yesterday, it is worthy of being placed on record, there was not one single spectator in Court. This, too, we believe, is a unique occurrence.

Irish Christian Advocate – 1922
"Revival in Lisburn " by Rev. J. N. Spence (Methodist Church)

Not within the memory of the oldest inhabitant has Lisburn been so deeply stirred as during the United Mission conducted by the Rev. W. P. Nicholson of Los Angeles. For the first ten days, Mr. Nicholson's sermons were addressed to Christians emphasising the necessity for the baptism of the Holy Spirit as a separable and separate blessing. With true Methodist emphasis, the doctrine was enforced and many hundreds claimed the promise of the life abundant. Night after night it was a thrilling sight to see scores of men and women, old and young, spring to their feet in response to the missioner's appeal for instant decision for Christ, and with uplifted hand shout "I will." Mr. Nicholson is blessedly unconventional in his methods, saying daring things, using blunt words, but all combining to give a vividness and fire to the message which rams it home to conscience and heart.

It is still far too early to speak of the ultimate results of the mission. Well over 2,000 souls definitely pledged themselves to Jesus Christ. 1,950 were dealt with in the enquiry room; over 700 names were transferred to the minister of one church in Lisburn, a number which actually out numbers the normal seating capacity of the building. All other churches have had large numbers of their members converted. In the congregations of our circuit almost 100 persons have professed conversion.

Powerfully as the numbers speak, the changed atmosphere of the town is an even more striking testimony. It is not too much to say that the entire community has been brought face to face with the question "What shall I do with Jesus?" In market and shop, in factory and workroom, in public house and club, in the villa and in the slum, in street and train, in fact everywhere the mission has been the constant subject of conversation.

There have been some very practical illustrations of the effect of the mission. Business people have had debts, long since written off as irrecoverable, paid in full. Money wrongfully used has been returned. At the last Petty Sessions Court there was only one case down for trial and the man concerned lives some miles out of Lisburn, a unique experience. There has been a great diversity in the types of character reached. Drunkards and gamblers have had the chains of their sins snapped. Formalists have been quickened into new life. A holy concern has gripped and changed the careless.

Two classes have been roused to bitter anger – the Pharisees and the publicans –a sure sign the Holy Spirit is working. It was not only in the meetings that conversions took place; many decided for Christ in the street or in their homes. One man, the son of godly parents, was under deep conviction of sin for weeks, but stubbornly declined to yield to Christ. In the middle of the night he awoke in overpowering concern about his soul, and yielding at last he awoke his wife to tell her the joyful news. The whole movement was aptly described by one of our godly members when she said, "It was a miracle that was happening in Lisburn."

Tribute from Local Ministers

Following the Lisburn Mission a tribute to the work of Mr. Nicholson appeared in The Lisburn Standard signed by the ministers J. J. C. Breakey, W. P. Carmody, J. N. Spence, R. W. Hamilton and T. G. Keery *(Extract)*.

'In the Rev. W. P. Nicholson we have a most able and efficient evangelist. A man of extraordinary gifts, strong and attractive personality with a wonderful experience and wide knowledge of life and men.... the originality of the missioner, his graphic and vivid presentation of the truth have aroused emotions, hostile and friendly; but criticism has served the Divine purpose and has been the means of furthering the Gospel, while the throngs which have waited upon the ministry of the Word and the number who have crowded the enquiry room prove that the power of God has been with His servant and are the best justification of his methods.

'Whilst in our midst, Mr. Nicholson has been in labours more abundant, giving himself without stint to the work of the Mission. To him we are most grateful and thank God for sending him amongst us. We earnestly pray that more and more he may be the honoured instrument in the salvation of multitudes. We feel it is only fair to Mr. Nicholson to say, that in coming to us he made no stipulation as to remuneration, fully content to accept the free-will gifts of the people of God.'

1923

RAVENHILL PRESBYTERIAN CHURCH
During the Mission of 1923 the central gate pillar was moved from its position by the crush of men trying to get in.

(From: 'Ravenhill Presbyterian Church
1898-1998' – Centenary History by Ivan T. Jess)

RAVENHILL PRESBYTERIAN CHURCH
Mission 11th February - 11th March 1923

When the 1923 mission in Ravenhill was arranged the church committee, conscious of the large enthusiastic crowds such meetings attracted, decided to protect the church building from possible damage. The windows on the inside were shielded and the main doors, formerly hinged, were replaced by sliding doors that gave easier access to the narrow vestibule.

The Rev. Harry Magill provides the following eye witness account (Contact Magazine No. 34 April 1973).

......"In his preaching he appealed especially to men and his meetings for men only were always packed and he used to say "not a woman put your nose round the door." Those who accepted Christ at his sessions included students, teachers, doctors and a goodly number of successful business men. Many who came to criticise stopped to pray. Those who professed faith in Christ proved the reality of their faith by their deeds many making restitution by paying old debts which business people had written off as unrecoverable.

Harland and Wolff had to build a special shed to hold all the returned stolen property.

It was a great privilege to be present in Ravenhill Presbyterian Church on the night of the march of the 'Island men.' They marched from Harland and Wolff in their dungarees and filled the church to capacity, the crush moving one of the outside pillars. Over one hundred men decided for Christ and it was a great thrill to see men standing in the pews tearing up bookmakers dockets, a sight never to be forgotten.

Someone summed up Mr. Nicholson by saying "he was the best loved and best hated man in Ulster," loved by all evangelical Christians and hated by the enemies of Christ.

The Rev. John Ross was asked "do Mr. Nicholson's converts stand?" He replied, "No, they go on."

In "God's Faithfulness" he recounts" .... a special march was arranged from the Queen's Island. The men had promised to come direct from their work to the church in their working clothes."

Rev. John Ross

Thousands came along and when they arrived at the church, unfortunately the gates were closed. When they were opened the crowd was so large that the men got wedged between the pillars, and so fierce was the struggle to get in that the central pillar was moved from its place. In a very short time the church was crowded to its utmost capacity with still an immense crowd outside...That same evening more than 100 men passed through the enquiry room, many of them making definite decisions for Christ.

The March of the Island Men

What means that eager, curious throng
Which lines the streets and waits so long?
And what went ye out to see
The Island men in dungarees?
These are the men that have been won
For Christ by Pastor Nicholson.
Make way, make way, you hear the cry,
And let the Island men pass by.

They come, they come, you hear them sing,
And loud their song of praises ring,
Belfast is very glad to see
Her men from bondage are set free.
While shouts of praises fill the air,
The devil leaves them in despair,
And once again you hear the cry,
The Island men are passing by.

No bullets fly, no bombs explode,
For Jesus leads them on the road,
Peace is proclaimed, and all is well,
The devil slopes off down to hell.
And that's the place to keep him low,
Down in the dumps we'll never go.
Make way, make way, you hear the cry,
And let the Island men pass by.

Oh wondrous change, what can it be
That moves this city mightily?
Give God the praise, for He alone
Can melt the heart as hard as stone.
Oh why will ye procrastinate?
Tomorrow you may be too late,
Join up, join up, why will ye die?
While Christ the Lord is passing by.

(Composed by an Island man)

A memory of W. P. Nicholson

On February 21, 1923, as a young man of 22, while residing at 30 Calvin Street in the East End of Belfast, God entered my life.

Hearing music, I remarked to my mother: "What on earth is a band doing out at this time of the year; it is not the Twelfth?"

"No," said my mother, "It is a Salvation Army band leading the converts of the Nicholson Revival meetings direct from the Shipyards to Ravenhill Presbyterian church."

"A bunch of fools," I replied in my ignorance, but some minutes later I was dressed and outside at the street corner soliciting information as to the route of the converts.

When I reached the church, a large crowd had gathered, and the brickwork supporting the railings gave way to the surging crowd. Carried forward with it, I entered this well-known church for the first time, lucky to obtain a seat.

There sat the Island men still in their overalls, some eating a sandwich. They were singing as only Irishmen can. "What a change has been wrought since Jesus came into my heart."

I do not remember what the Rev. W. P. Nicholson preached on that evening, but, during the most manly act of my life, I joined the rest of the awakened sinners, and made a commitment to God.

James Doggart (Canada)
(Belfast Telegraph Letters - March 1973)

From: "A Local Perspective" – W. P. Nicholson by Ken McFall

CARRICKFERGUS UNITED MISSION

An application for the use of First Presbyterian Church was lodged on the 16th November 1922 on behalf of "United Missions" in the name of Rev. W. P. Nicholson.

Following a specially convened Session meeting, the Minister in charge, Rev. Alexander Cuthbert, presided and after the application received its due considerations, it was agreed to loan the church for a mission to be held in the following Spring, 1923.

From that moment the necessary preparations began to take shape in readiness for the Servant of God. It proved to be a mission that would be long remembered as a time of refreshing from the Lord.

An account shows that two ladies washed and scrubbed the church from end to end. They were instructed that the water used must be disinfected, and that the work would, on completion, be inspected by the appointed committee. The hire charge for the two ladies was ten shillings per day. The church took seven days to make ready.

The hiring and carriage of a piano from M. Crymble Ltd., Wellington Place, Belfast, came to five pounds and five shillings for the duration of the five week mission. The local firm of E. Caters, Irish Quarter West, fitted boards to the church windows, removed umbrella holders, raised a platform in the pulpit and removed pew cushions etc.

Advertising the Mission proved the most costly. Carrickfergus Advertiser and East Antrim Gazette advertised the mission weekly, in addition to printing two hundred handbills announcing the prayer meeting and a further two thousand leaflets printed for distribution throughout the town.

By the time Carrickfergus had the privilege of hearing God's Servant, with God's message, a lot of stories were beginning to filter out and circulate the town.

Already in Carrickfergus the town's people had on their minds all that they heard from the other meetings, but very soon the name "Nicholson" would be on their lips.

There were great expectations when the meetings commenced and when Nicholson mounted the pulpit there was the feeling of the nearness of God in the service, in the prayers, in the hymn singing and the power of God felt in the preaching of the Gospel of Christ. Each morning in Carrick the conversation was about the Mission and centred on who had been converted the night before. A rush of curiosity gripped the town as the nightly meetings continued and capacity crowds swamped the church building in eagerness to find a seat. Every morning a greater attention would be drawn to the work being done by the power of God as the question, "What do you think of Nicholson?" was being asked by the people in the streets.

The hymn and chorus singing from the Alexander's Hymns No. 3 rang out each night. From the outset Rev. Nicholson selected a volley of lively hymns which would be instantly recognised by the congregation who could sing them with the hymn book closed.

Some of those hymns included:

431 *O happy day, O happy day, when Jesus washed my sins away*
 70 *When the trumpet of the Lord shall sound, and time shall be no more*
  4 *I stand amazed in the presence of Jesus the Nazarene*
169 *Would you be free from your burden of sin?*

These are only four of the many favourites. Normally the singing at the close of the meeting would conclude with Nicholson's own Anthem!

> *"Down in the dumps I'll never go,*
> *That's where the devil keeps me low,*
> *So I'll sing with all my might*
> *And I'll keep my armour bright,*
> *But – down in the dumps I'll never go."*

Each evening before the meeting commenced, enthusiastic hymn singing could be heard as the congregation waited for Nicholson to arrive. Then when the meeting concluded and the crowds spilled out on to the street, the hymn singing never seemed to cease.

One Thousand Souls

The First Presbyterian Church saw the building packed night by night with capacity crowds for the duration of the five week mission.

At the end of the campaign many had professed to have accepted Christ as a personal Saviour while others were stirred by the powerful appeals of the preacher. An average of two hundred souls each week were born again by the Spirit of God and only eternity will reveal the true worth and value of this mission.

The local Carrickfergus Advertiser carried this report of the mission.

Carrickfergus Advertiser – May 1923

The United Mission conducted by Rev. W. P. Nicholson, of Los Angeles, in the First Presbyterian Church, Carrickfergus, continues to attract large congregations. The preacher's blunt and unpolished way of delivering his message is certainly resented by many. It is the method of John Knox and Martin Luther and other reformers, who recognised that there are people to whom the plain simple story makes little or no appeal, and times when the stern realities of the case must be presented, if Christianity is not to degenerate into a pulseless, fibreless inert affair, more social than soul saving, and with a decreasing weakening influence. If there are those who dislike the methods of the man, and admittedly there are many, there are hundreds to whom he has been a revelation, a voice crying in the wilderness, calling for repentance with a voice such as they had never heard. The message may be delivered in uncultured language, it may sometimes have more of the atmosphere of the stokehold than the university about it, but it brings with it the tonic effect of the strong sea breeze rather than the enervation of the sultry plain. It is a message to be delivered, and the speaker sees that it is delivered, and if it is unsuitable for the delicate appetites of some it suits the constitutional needs of as many more.

A typical meeting was held on Tuesday:

There was a large number of visitors from the City of Belfast, where wonderful results have been obtained, and these people came down full of glowing enthusiasm which is simply unaccountable to those not acquainted with the work. The service commenced at eight, but for an hour before, the Church was crowded and the missioner kept his congregation busily engaged singing hymns, whistling and humming, and they entered lustily into the spirit of it all. Then, as eight o'clock approached, one after another of these young fellows and girls got up and voluntarily testified to their experience, giving in every case the date and place of their conversion.

"That's good," said Mr. Nicholson, "you all know the place and date of your natural birth, and why shouldn't you know the place and date of your spiritual birth?" About twenty persons had declared themselves for Christ at the meeting on the night before and the missioner set his Carrick converts a difficult task.

Wee Carrick

"I want you," he said, "to stand up here and now and testify for Christ. Mind you, I know that's a very hard thing to ask, and a harder to do. It was easy enough in Belfast, where one might live beside a man for twenty years and not know him, but in wee Carrick it's different. Here, or in Bangor, if you want to know your own business, or how you are getting on, as your neighbour, ask the man or women next door. But there should be no sneaks in religion. It's straight clean duty. If it's something to be ashamed of don't say a word about it, but if it's nothing to be ashamed of to belong to Christ and His Church, for God's sake don't be ashamed to let the world know it."

The appeal was not without effect and a good proportion of the local converts bravely stood up in view of that great congregation, and publicly testified to their entry into Grace.

The Final Account of the Mission

After the final hymn was sung and the benediction pronounced, God had richly poured out his blessings upon the people of this town, especially for the hundreds who had been changed by the power of God.

One of the converts spoke of his entire family coming to Christ. Today he said it is different. Few are the cases where there is household salvation, but they had all learned that the old account of their souls was paid for on Calvary. The mission also revealed that God was no man's debtor, for as the income was tallied with the expenditure there was a substantial balance in favour of God's work.

Belfast Telegraph 1923

Island men and the Missioner
East Belfast Episode
End of the Nicholson Crusade

Undoubtedly, Mr. Nicholson is a very unique personality. He is a law unto himself. Whilst many will question some of his methods and phrases in his speeches, he has been signally used by the Most High in arousing careless men and women to think of better things.

So said the Right Rev. Dr. Henry Montgomery, ex-Moderator of the General Assembly, in an interesting conversational account of his impressions of the Nicholson mission, which had so conspicuously successful a culminating finale at the mass meetings in St. Enoch's Church and the Albert Hall, Shankhill Road, on Wednesday afternoon and evening.

Rev. Dr Montgomery cordially received the "Telegraph" Representative in his office at the Albert Hall, the approach to which bears the welcoming motto, "Be of Good Cheer." He is well qualified to speak on the subject of revival and mission work, having had the privilege of being secretary for the late Mr. D. L. Moody on the occasions of three visits of that great evangelist to Belfast; also acting in a similar capacity for Rev. Dr. Torrey and the late Mr. Alexander, also for the late Rev. Dr. Chapman, with whom Mr. Alexander, of "Glory" hymn fame was colleague.

"In the days of Mr. Moody's splendid work," Dr. Montgomery said, "splendid work was done of a unique character, and many young men, were influenced to enter the ministry, who are now doing fine service in different churches."

Dr. Torrey's visit appealed to a different type. He was logical and theological in his mode of address, and appealed to a different type of mind from those influenced by Mr. Moody.

"Dr. Chapman was tender and gracious in his public ministry, and struck a keynote different from the earlier evangelists."

Great Crowds Everywhere

As to the Rev. W. P. Nicholson, whose strenuous career in Ulster is, for the present, coming to a close, has during the last two and a half years conducted great evangelistic campaigns in some fifteen or sixteen centres in Northern Ireland areas. Wherever he has gone great crowds have flocked to his ministry, so that no building, however large its capacity, was capable of containing the crowds who sought to hear and learn from him.

"His ministry, when at any given centre, consisted generally speaking, of three services every Sunday, one every week-night, whilst three afternoons of each week were usually devoted to Bible Talks. In the case of St. Enoch's Church and of the Albert Hall the afternoon meetings comfortably filled those spacious buildings, and the same was experienced in most of the centres in which he worked. Then, on the closing Sunday at each place he visited he generally spoke five different times on the same day.

"One wonders how the physical effort did not altogether incapacitate the preacher at some time or other, but he always came up fresh and fervent. He took an interval of six days' rest between his work in the different areas, and this, no doubt, helped to sustain his strength and energy.

No Use for the Choir

"In his services Mr. Nicholson neither desired choir nor choir leader. Once he got 'on the bridge' he was captain and remained there in charge, leading the praise service, preaching, and conducting the after-meeting. These services lasted generally three hours, and it was extraordinary how the freshness of them never relaxed in any way.

"Mr. Nicholson's after-meetings were conducted in his own special way. Everyone was asked to express his or her interest in better things by rising to their feet and later making their way to one of the smaller halls or rooms set apart for enquirers."

The Albert Hall

In the case of the Albert Hall, men were met with in one room, women in another and boys and girls in a third. Mr. Nicholson took no part in these personal enquiry meetings, which were in charge of local ministers, assisted by members of the various congregations. It is only fair to say that vast influence, so far as one can judge, has been made, and many have been deeply impressed for good by the fervent ministrations of Mr. Nicholson, supported by his co-workers in the different centre.

"His style is breezy and naturally. The early career of Mr. Nicholson at sea has given him that free and easy manner beloved of the humbler classes.

"He has a remarkable vocabulary of powerful, pungent English, and is never at a loss for a word.

"He has got a clear grip of Scripture, which has a wonderful hold upon him.

"He sticks to his Bible with great tenacity, and gives chapter and verse for all his utterances.

"In my judgement" (the worthy head of the Albert Hall continued, his face illumined with fervid enthusiasm as he discussed the great Bangor-born missioner) "Mr. Nicholson presents the gospel in a gripping and powerful and tremendously earnest way.

"There are many of us associated with him in the Mission who have known men come in to scoff and remain to pray; and others who came to criticise – having heard rumours about his 'rough speech' have been captured by his cheery, happy methods.

"His language, on occasion, can be very strong, and many people are known to think it unnecessarily rough, as well as severe. Mr. Nicholson, however, does not ask any of those interested in his meetings to endorse his mode of speech or his sledgehammer blows at what he considers great moral or social evils.

"He stands on his own and vindicates his own language.

"Ministers of all denominations have rallied round him because of the manifest results of his ministry during the two and a half years he has been working in this Northern area of ours.

"Whilst he has many who differ from him and are averse to his modes of speech, as well as of his strong criticisms of individuals, he yet leaves behind him tens of thousands of men, women, and young people who love him with a warm affection.

By Charabanc to Ballymena

"It is well known that Queen's Island men have left the shipyards in their dungarees to drive by charabancs as far as Ballymena, their wives meeting them at the gates to give them flasks of hot tea and other refreshments which they could use on the way to this populous and industrious mid-Antrim town.

"The evangelist who is capable of producing a result like that has 'something to him' which needs to be accounted for.

"It will be remembered that while Mr. Nicholson was preaching in the Newtownards Road Methodist Church, some time ago, so great was the crush of Island men to get in that they carried the gates away with them; and that on that particular night 240 men were dealt with about their interest in Jesus Christ. They also agreed at the time to compensate the damage done to the structure, and before Mr. Nicholson leaves on his return to America the gates are to be re-dedicated, having been strengthened and restored to a condition for their proper use by the Methodist congregation. Mr. Nicholson, will, I believe, take part in that interesting service."

Asked concerning Mr. Nicholson's future movements, Rev. Dr. Montgomery said he expected he would be sailing by the Clyde shipping Company's steamer for London from Belfast on 23rd inst., his preference – after so many years at sea – being for a long voyage rather than a train journey. It is probably that his last meeting in the city will be at Newington Presbyterian Church on Monday night next.

He has visited almost all the centres in which he has held missions to have farewell services.

"Yesterday" (said the ex-Moderator), "he asked that the collections at the farewell services in St. Enoch's and Albert Hall, though not for his own use, should be at his own disposal to hand over to a fund for the building of a large Union Evangelistic Hall in Bangor – (place of his birth and where he was brought up). The collections from the two centres are expected to reach £100.

"Mr. Nicholson will resume his evangelical work in Los Angeles, on the Pacific coast – a city of over 800,000 inhabitants – in August next. The friends there are putting up a large and substantial wooden auditorium specially for his meetings, capable of accommodating 5,000 people, so that the evangelist has evidently more strenuous days before him.

"It is not always that a son of the soil has attracted so much popular favour when on his native heath, as has been the case with Mr. Nicholson. Most of the men who have made their mark in this City, for example, have been of foreign origin; but there we have seen great and lasting results from the work of a man born and brought up in loyal County Down.

"Mr. Nicholson always speaks of the places of his birth with pleasure and pride. He took a strong view of the political difficulties of Ulster a few years ago, and was never backward in professing his profound convictions as to the effects of Home Rule. He still stands four-square for the Union. But while that is so he is, first and last, a powerful Gospel preacher; and if ever he comes back to the North of Ireland – as we hope he and Mrs. Nicholson will – there are multitudes who will heartily welcome their return."

Rev. John Pollock, Rev. William Maguire, and other ministers took part in the farewell service at St. Enoch's Church on Wednesday afternoon. Mr. Nicholson, in his address thanked Mr. Pollock and the members of the church for the assistance they had given him in carrying on his mission. He expressed the great delight it had given him to preach in his native land, and said he believed they were only at the beginning of the good work, and that greater achievements lay ahead. He went on to say how the results, of the mission work could be retained when the campaign was over and those who were converted went back to other common round and daily task. He urged them to be dead to the things of the world, but alive to every appeal of God; and counselled them not to worry, which was in itself, a sin.

There was an overflowing congregation in the Albert Hall at night. Right Rev. Dr. Montgomery presided, and Rev. John Pollock, W. R. Sloan, John Ross, Samuel Simms,

John Milliken, W. P. McVitty. H. Frackleton, H. Deale, and Pastor Hodgett (Ballymena) were amongst the ministers present. Dr. Montgomery said they had met to express their gratitude to God for the visit of his servants, Mr. and Mrs. Nicholson, and for the wonderful way in which He had used them to promote His cause in Northern Ireland. They desired to give to them some expression of their gratitude for the herculean work they had done during what must have been the most strenuous period of their busy lives. (hear hear). God had endowed them with spiritual qualifications to carry on a great and good work leading multitudes of people to know Christ and stimulating the Christian life and more accurate and helpful service. They were met to wish Mr. Nicholson and his wife God-speed in their journey across the ocean, and to tell them that if they came back there would be thousands of hearts to welcome them. They rejoiced in Mr. Nicholson" fidelity to the Word of God and the moral and spiritual strength of his ministry. He used no flattering phrases or honeyed expressions, and he had given offence to some who resented the strong language they thought he used. But he (Dr. Montgomery) did not think that any of the language was stronger than the language of Christ or John the Baptist. The language of the Scriptures was plain, and could not be misunderstood.

Rev. W. R. Sloan then read the following address:-

To the Rev. Wm. P. Nicholson, at the close of a long and very successful evangelistic campaign in Ulster, 1921-1923:

ALBUM WITH ILLUMINATED ADDRESS
(From 'Alliance News' magazine of the Irish Alliance of Christian Workers Unions)

Dear Mr. Nicholson

We cannot allow you to leave the shores of your native Ulster without letting you know how much tens of thousands who have profited by your faithful and untiring labours in the Gospel in many centres over this northern land admire and love you for your work's sake.

You came amongst us as a faithful ambassador of the Cross, and with a good record behind you of splendid services rendered for Christ in many lands, including Australia and the United States. Now there are thousands in our own land who regard you with warm affection as being the honoured instrument of their salvation through faith in Jesus Christ. We believe, however, that God anointed you with a double portion of His Spirit for the great work to which he called you in Ulster.

Here in this your native province vast multitudes have waited on your ministry, which for fervour, for spirituality, for fidelity to the Word of God, for pungency of expression and for gripping speech has seldom, if ever been excelled in this country.

But we specially rejoice that whilst your ministry has fallen like showers upon the parched land for Christians, it has been eminently blessed in leading thousands of men and women and young people to accept Jesus Christ as their Saviour and to enlist under His banner for His service and glory.

Rev. and Mrs. W. P. Nicholson
(the former Miss Ellison D. Marshall of
Bellshill, Lanarkshire). They were married in 1907.

We recognise with warmest gratitude that you have found in Mrs. Nicholson so true a help-meet (when she was able to render them) in connection with the great campaign now closing have been as acceptable as your own. She, too, has been used of God for leading many into the light and liberty of the gospel.

It is impossible to tabulate by mere words the deep and abiding spiritual influences that have been brought into being through your instrumentality. Ulster wears a new look today because of what God has permitted you to do amongst us. "The voice of rejoicing and salvation is in the tabernacles of the righteous: for the right hand of the Lord has done valiantly."

Whilst we thank your dear wife and yourself with all our hearts for what the Lord has enabled you to do for Him and His cause here, we give God all the glory.

It is a great delight to us to think of the new bond of loving Christian union that has been established between you and ourselves which nothing can dissolve.

You will live in the hearts of multitudes of God's redeemed people in this land so long as life and memory shall last.

Because of this bond we now invite you to return to our shores as soon as the Pillar cloud moves in our direction, and assure you to a very hearty welcome.

Prevented by you from offering any very tangible expression of our gratitude and affection, we beg your kind acceptance of this Album, with the names of representatives from the various centres in Ulster where your faithful and fruitful ministry has been exercised.

We remain,
Affectionately yours in Gospel fellowship,

Henry Montgomery, Chairman
E. B. Cullen
H. Stephens Richardson
James Soye
H. Livingstone Junior
W. R. Sloan
R. Nimmon
S. G. Montgomery, Hon. Secretary
Thomas Bailie, Asst. Hon. Secretary

June 13th 1923

After the address and the signatures, a number of pages are devoted to the various missions held over the period during which Mr. Nicholson was in Ulster. These pages have illustrations depicting some aspect of the places concerned, and signatures of representatives are appended.

For the **Bangor Mission**, the following signatures appear:
James F. Brice, Thomas Bailie, James T. Brice, Thomas Cooper, Davis Harvey, Jennie Hanna, W. A. Hill, James Hutchinson, John McClure, A. N. McDowell, R. J. Morrell, S. G. Montgomery, Edward Nelson, Samuel Owens, John N. Spence, W. J. Wilson.

Derry City Mission:
R. Nimmon, Joseph C. Eaton, R. D. Gordon, John A. Pollock, J. Golligher, W. A. Weir, A. H. Graham, T. H. Thompson, Robert Grandsden.

Sandy Row and Donegall Road:
Thomas A. Smyth, Robert Anderson, A. C. Browne, Wm. Fulton, J. B. McClean, Archibald Irwin, George E. Howe.

Shipyard Workers:
John Mackay, John Atkinson, Thomas Kirk, John Ward, Robert Auld.

Ballymagarrett Mission:
John Redmond, W. Presley McVitty C. S. Greeves, A. Jardine, James Norman Law, James H. Brown, Joseph Howe.

Lurgan Mission:
Anthony Bunting. H. Livingstone Jun., Thomas Baxter, Wm. H. E. Brown, Fred A. Ferguson, Samuel Metcalfe, Edward Ferguson, Wm. Henry Campbell, James Soye.

Portadown Mission:
J. H. Stevenson, R. W. Willis, S. Fergus, R. M. Woods, Jas. Bryson, George Johnston, Capel W. Reid, Samuel S. Corbett, W. J. Moffett, William Fitsimons.

Shankhill Road Mission:
Henry Montgomery, D. D., John McCready, Elizabeth Martin, David Sands, Elizabeth Hume, R. J. McIlroy, David Irwin, Thomas George Hunter, J. Milliken, Edward Hazelton, W. J. Calvin, J. B. Wallace, James Gault, Samuel Simms.

North Belfast Christian Workers Union:
Leila L. Dunlop, Elizabeth Montgomery, John Moore, Edwin A. Montgomery, J. C. Sherry.

Postmen
(Postmen's text "The posts went with the letters from the king" - 2 Chronicles 30: 6)
R. J. Aiken, Robt. Johnston, Wm. J. Gray, W. Johnston, Wm. James Scott.

Tramwaymen:
John Montgomery, Thomas Henry Moore, Robert Burniston, Henry Reains, Hugh Graham, John Dawson.

Ravenhill Road Mission:
John Ross, James L. Harbinson, Samuel Bailie, Thomas H. Watson.

St. Enoch's Church Mission:
John Pollock, Johnstone Hunter, W. George Forsythe, Edward Wightman, John Currie, Wm. A. Sinclair, R. A. Gray, D. P. Connery.

Ballymena Mission:
John Armstrong Cullen, W. J. Hanson, Henry Frackelton, William Millar, R. M. McCheyne Gilmour, Hugh A. Dunlop, Richard Hodgett.

Newtownards Mission
Wm. E. Maguire, W. R. Sloan, James Holmes, James Apperson, Robert Edgar, M. H. Walker, William Duncan, Thos. A. Reid, Samuel Bradley, Emily Wilson.

Carrickfergus Mission:
Alexander Cuthbert, James McDowell, Robert Rodgers, Samuel Jenkins, W. C. Jones, S. Mains Shaw, John Armstrong, E. B. Cullen, J. Donaldson, Robert James Taylor, Charles M. Legg.

Newington Church Mission:

Thomas M. Johnstone, William J. Clarke, Joseph Millar, John Hamilton, James Mateer, Andrew Mulholland.

Dromore Mission:

Robert Acheson, J. A. Doak, George Ervine, E. J. Dowie, James Ervine, H. J.F. Ranson, Thomas Murphy, Thos. Geo. Pritchard.

Rosemary St., Men's School Mission:

Sam Brown, Wm. Lutton, F. J. Holland, Florence Holland, Samuel Graham, John Green, D. Lyle Hall, S.J.G. Park.

Lisburn Mission:

R.H.S. Cooper, J.J. Carlyle Breakey, James Morrow, James McNally, Samuel B. McCleery, Mary Neill, Robert Bannister, W. P. Carmody, R. W. Hamilton, Thomas Haire, James Shortt, Fred. H. Menary, Florrie Wilson, Wm. J. Wilson.

Rev. W.P. Nicholson (Standing) with two senior colleagues

Rev. W. P. NICHOLSON'S MISSION

—- oOo —-

THE LORD HATH DONE GREAT THINGS FOR US;
WHEREOF WE ARE GLAD.   Psalm cxxvi, 3.

To make another poem
I am too old a man,
But I must speak out for God and truth
And do the best I can.

God has sent His servant here,
He has crossed the mighty deep
To cry aloud, wake up Belfast!
For you are fast asleep.

And he has blessed his message.
For he had God's truth to tell,
And thousands have been led to see
They were on the way to hell.

Give God all the Glory
For by Him this work was done;
And may every awakened sinner
Trust in His dear Son.

For Christ can save the Gunmen,
Whose sins were crimson dyed,
Who in their Hell-born zeal –
All Heaven's laws defied.

He can save the chief of sinners,
If they all trust in Him;
For the Blood He shed on Calvary
Can wash away their sins.

This is a blessed time –
Oh, it makes the Angels sing!
When many give up the Devil,
And take Christ as Lord and King.

O sinner, will you take Jesus,
O do it, here and now –
Say in your heart I will take Jesus,
Dear Lord to Thee I bow.

Many are singing with all their hearts -
As they never sang before –
Praising Him who gave them Life;
Yes Life for evermore!

And their songs have set the Devil mad,
He has now began to cry,
You might hear Him at Rosemary Street
If you are passing by.

To crush this great man Nicholson,
All Hell are now combined;
But they never will be able,
For His God is Strong and Kind.

His Captain is the Son of God,
He will the Devil smite,
But he will come off victorious
For this is Heaven's fight.

The Devil has His Agents,
I can meet them every day;
But they are such awful liars
Believe not what they say.

Their Father is a Liar
The Truth He never told;
Eve could tell you that –
For she knew the boy of old.

But go and hear that man of God,
Make haste and almost run –
For as a Preacher of Christ's Gospel
He is second now to none.

Thank God, we have Ministers –
Yes many in Belfast,
Who have stood by Mr. Nicholson,
And defend him to the last.

Lord send us more such Ministers,
To this our native land;
Men full of love and pity –
Who for God and truth would stand.

Men like Doctor Cook,
Who threw away his gown,
And never gave up the fight,
Till he put the rebels down.

We need a Champion for the Faith;
For many are led astray
For the Mormon's and Russelism –
Of the present day.

Nicholson is a Champion –
He has fought the Devil well;
He has let the Unitarians know
They are marching down to hell.

If they want to get to Heaven
They must go by Heaven's plan;
Redemption through the Blood
For Lord and Ruined man.

If your Minister in the Pulpit,
Says there is any other way;
If you tell him he's a liar –
It is the proper thing to say.

A great Campaign is on the move,
It's coming like a flood
To sweep us all to Heaven –
Without the Saviour's Blood.

The Old Serpent is the Leader,
He has led them all their days;
He will do His best to blind you all;
Don't believe a word He says.

Child of God before I close,
Just a word for you –
Keep trusting in your Saviour –
For nothing else will do.

Begin and work for God-
Don't wait another day
Ask the Lord to help you –
He will teach you what to say.

You may not speak like Angels,
You may not Preach like Paul;
But you can tell the love of Jesus
You can say He Died for All.

W. Watson, 16 Avonbeg St., Belfast.

1924

News Letter 31st July 1924

REV. W. P. NICHOLSON AT BANGOR
Welcomed at Public Meeting

The Rev. W. P. Nicholson, the well-known evangelist who conducted a revival campaign in Belfast and various parts of Ulster last year, was welcomed on his return visit at a crowded meeting in the Hamilton Road Presbyterian Church, Bangor, last night. Prior to the meeting, at which Mr. S. G. Montgomery presided, tea was provided at the Guildhall. On entering the pulpit Mr. Nicholson had a rousing reception, and the congregation sang the Doxology.

The Chairman said that on Sunday next Mr. Nicholson would visit Whiteabbey, and in the course of the next few months he would conduct meetings at Magherafelt, Ulsterville Church, Belfast, Portglenone, Donaghadee, and Whitehead or Bessbrook.

Addresses of welcome were delivered by Mr. S. G. Montgomery, representing the Bangor Christian Workers Society, Rev. R. J. Morrell, Trinity Presbyterian Church, Rev. W. J. Wilson, Queen's Parade Methodist Church, Rev. W. H. Hill, Hamilton Road Presbyterian Church, Rev. H. Montgomery, D.D., Shankhill Road Mission, Belfast; Rev. John Ross, Ravenhill Presbyterian Church, Belfast, Pastor Jardin, Grove Hall, Belfast, Rev. Samuel Simms, North Belfast Christian Workers Union, Mr. J. B. McLean, Irish organiser of the Faith Mission, Mr. Arch. Irwin, J.P. Cripples Institute, Belfast and Bangor; Mr. Mackay, Shipyard Workers' Christian Union, Mr. Moore, Tramwaymen's Christian Union, Mr. John Simpson, East Belfast Christian Workers' Union, Mr. James Mairs, Donaghadee, Rev. Wm. McVitty, Donaghadee, Mr. Joseph Goligher, Londonderry, Mr. Stevenson, Portadown, Rev. William Maguire, Antrim, Mr. Reid, Newtownards and Mr. Magill, Carrowdore.

Mr. Nicholson said it was hard for him to express the feelings of joy and delight which Mrs. Nicholson and himself had experienced by the cordial welcome extended to them. Since 19th May he had travelled six thousand miles and preached two or three times a day in Canada and the United States. If ever he got a surprise it was when he was called back to Ulster when work was opening up in other places.

During the year Mrs. Nicholson and he were in America they travelled twenty thousand miles in working for the Lord, but it came upon their minds that He would have them back again in Ulster. He believed it was an answer to the prayers of those whom he had bade good-bye a year ago. They were brought back by God, and the gates of hell would not prevail against them.

The Lord had been gracious unto them as they had had the pleasure of seeing a large number of the people won for Him in Canada and America, and on their way back to Ulster they had received messages of welcome even when they were five or six hundred miles at sea.

But if anything were to be accomplished here they would require to keep their eyes on God, because without Him they could do nothing. But let them all pray that God might sweep across the border and touch their brethren who were in the bonds of Roman Catholicism.

Mr. Nicholson then proceeded to deliver the message which, he said, had been laid upon his heart before leaving America, his text being taken from John 10. 15-18. Christ, he said, came to die, and He taught them to die. To day the emphasis was on life, whereas in Christ's teaching it was on death, and the curse of modern theology was the sanctification of character.

Alliance News
MAGHERAFELT
"Prayer availeth much"

Magherafelt Christian Workers' Union was formed after Mr. Nicholson had a mission in the town in September 1924. We had a mighty awakening whilst God's servant was in our midst, very many lives, especially young men, were led to accept Christ as their Saviour. We praise God for sending Mr. Nicholson to us for he was used in reaching numbers who were "down and out" in sin of various kinds, drinking and gambling had taken hold of many of the young men, and now these same young men are not ashamed to get up in the open air or in the meetings of the Union, and testify to the power of Christ in their lives to keep them from these evils to which they were formerly in bondage. It is delightful to hear them praying and saying "O Lord, we thank You for sending Your servant Mr. Nicholson to our town, and for using him to awaken us. Bless him wherever he goes."

We had been praying before the mission – yes, for years before – that God would raise up a band of young men who would not be ashamed to go along the country roads, singing the praises of our God, and now He has done it, and we thank Him and take courage, looking for greater showers of blessing than we yet have experienced. "By the word of the Lord were the heavens made; and all the host of them by the breath of His mouth; for He spake and it was done; He commanded and it stood fast." And our God Who did all this is our Father in Christ Jesus, and to the cry of His children He will hearken, and so we are looking through the work of our Union, and the testimony and heart yearnings of His children here, that He will deluge our town and district with floods of blessing from Himself.

1925

COUNTY DOWN SPECTATOR – 3rd January 1925

THE REV. W. P. NICHOLSON
By the Very Rev. H. Montgomery, M.A., D.D.

The writer had a visit this summer from a successful Presbyterian minister in the State of Pennslyvania, U.S.A. In the course of conversation he said: "I see you have an evangelist on this side by the name of the Rev. W. P. Nicholson. I was present at his ordination a good many years ago now in the Presbytery of Carlisle, Penn., and had a share in the Ordination Act. He is a man who did great good in the evangelistic line all over that large area." This was unsolicited testimony from the other side of the Atlantic.

Invited to prepare a short article, recalling some of the salient points in connection with Mr. Nicholson's life, the writer has the advantage of having known his parents and grandparents on both sides with intimacy.

Mr. Nicholson comes of well-to-do Ulster Presbyterian Stock. His grandfather and grandmother were very regular worshippers in the congregation of the late Rev. W. Patteson, of Bangor, a godly and devoted minister of the gospel, who was often made a blessing to the present writer, and whose memory he cherishes with warm affection. Mr. and Mrs. Campbell (Mr. Nicholson's grandparents) were also warm friends of the minister, and one can recall the regularity with which they attended their place of worship on the Lord's Day, and particularly at the communion seasons. His grandfather (Captain Nicholson) was an earnest Christian man, devoted to prayer meetings and to any good work he could do. Whatever there may be in a worthy ancestry, the Rev. W. P. Nicholson can look back upon his fore-bearers with gratitude to God. He himself was called after the Rev. William Patteson. The family of Mr. Nicholson also attended upon the ministry of the present writer for a number of years during his pastorate in Albert Street Presbyterian Church, Belfast, and the years of the evangelist's boyhood are linked up with that congregation.

All these things, however, while good and helpful in themselves, were not enough, for as a youth, Mr. Nicholson fought shy of coming into contact with the pastor, whom he knew would speak to him on personal religion. The writer can recall at the close of a Sabbath evening service making for the place in which the lad sat, but before getting there he had quickly climbed over the side of the pew into the next one and made his way to the door down the opposite aisle. His early life was spent without any interest in the things that really matter and away from God. God, however, in His sovereign grace had mercy, and when still a young man, though with a very varied career behind him, he was led, in his own home, through the ministry of the Divine Spirit, to accept the Lord Jesus as his own personal Saviour. Led on step by step, he gradually developed marked gifts as a speaker. For Bible study he attended the Bible Training Institute in Glasgow for a year, but his restless nature and his passion for preaching the Gospel and seeking to win people back to God overcame him, and he launched out on what has proved to be his great life work, namely, the leading of sinners to the Saviour, by the proclamation of the unchanging message of life in Christ Jesus.

It may be mentioned that after Mr. Nicholson left the B.T.I. he was engaged as evangelist in connection with the Lanarkshire Christian Union, and in that capacity he did yeoman service in a tent. He also took charge of Pastor Findlay's Tabernacle for a year, when the Pastor and Mrs. Findlay were making a missionary tour in the East.

Mr. Nicholson has had considerable experience in evangelistic work in the Southern Hemisphere. He was linked up with Dr. Torrey and Mr. Alexander, and also with Dr. Chapman and Mr. Alexander, and his campaigns in Australia were greatly blessed of God. The late Mr. Alexander took a deep interest in Mr. Nicholson, and under his auspices the young evangelist had fellowship with Mr. Hemminger as his singer. They gradually branched out and conducted missions on their own, and undoubtedly the testimony of the young minister last summer was quite true when he stated that all over that vast area in Pennsylvania much blessing came. Mr. Nicholson was known not only as a rousing evangelist, but as the unsleeping foe of the drink evil. He organised what was called the "Anti-Booze" campaign in the various places he visited. Towns were stirred up to enthusiasm against the drink, and the trade organised opposition, so that many sleepy towns were aroused against the saloon as never before. He bears down on the drink curse in unmeasured terms of hostility wherever he goes.

In later years Mr. Nicholson has been very much in single harness. He has visited many parts of America, and has also been in Northern Ireland at different times. It was only, however, within the last three years that Mr. Nicholson, so to speak, came into his own. He began a series of meetings in Bangor that were a phenomenal success. From thence he went to Newtownards and was wonderfully blessed there also. The prophet was really having honour in his own country. Since then Mr. Nicholson has had campaigns in quite a number of centres in Belfast and in different parts of Ulster.

He has the ear of the people in a very remarkable degree; they crowd to hear him, and although Mr. Nicholson's sermons are often an hour long, they listen with the most eager interest from beginning to end. His sermons are thoroughly sound and Scriptural. He preaches the New birth, conversion the work of the Holy Spirit, and separation from the world, with great force. The Spirit of God has evidently rested upon him in much power, for he delivers to the people as he understands it, the whole counsel of God. He speaks of sin as the Bible views it; of Salvation as the Bible gives it, and of the power of the Gospel to deliver the slaves of evil from the cruel bondage for evermore. Mr. Nicholson is full of quaint humour, and is a master of racy speech. He has the power of apt illustration, and his gripping and telling words appeal to the crowd in a remarkable way. Just now he is continuing his work as an evangelist in different Ulster centres, and has engagements to keep him here well on to the end of 1925.

There are those who think that Mr. Nicholson's language is sometimes excessive and that he would do better work by using a more moderate form of speech. There are also those who would and indeed who would not be interested in his ministry. When, however, all these things have been said the fact remains that God has used the evangelist to do a great uplifting work in Ulster and far beyond it. Many men and women, young and old, have been led into the light and liberty of the Gospel. It is not for us to tabulate results, but one can truly say that to a multitude Mr. Nicholson has been a messenger of mercy and a minister of Jesus Christ.

It is only right to add that Mr. Nicholson's wife is a true helpmeet in the Lord. Her gentle and unobtrusive manner and her zeal in seeking to win her sisters for Jesus Christ endears her to all with whom she comes in contact. We may well thank God for both these faithful servants of our Lord and Saviour, and pray that God may use them more and more and grant them increasing wisdom and fervour in furthering the cause of evangelical religion in this Northern Land.

Alliance News
BESSBROOK C.W.U.

The C.W.U. was commenced shortly after the mission held by Rev. W. P. Nicholson in February 1925, fostered by the desire that evangelistic work should be encouraged along interdenominational lines, and we are very glad to report that there is much unity displayed in all our activities.

We have held an evangelistic service throughout the summer and winter, every Sunday night at 8.30, with encouraging attendance. Ministers and laymen have given their services willingly, and we believe that as the Gospel of our Lord and Saviour Jesus Christ has been preached in all its fullness and the way of salvation made plain, souls have been born again and have entered upon the Christian life.

BANGOR 1925
FAITH MISSION EASTER CONVENTION

FAITH MISSION GROUP AT EASTER CONVENTION 1925

Back Row: *Mr. J. B. McLean, Mr. Belford, Mr. Horace Govan, Mr. W. Millar,*
                    Mr. H. W. Verner, Mr. Gillespie, Mr. Angus McLean
Front Row: *Mr. W. P. Nicholson, Mr. and Mrs. J. G. Govan, Mr. A. Cumming.*

(From 'On Towards the Goal! (Nicholson))

The following is taken from one of the messages preached by Rev. W. P. Nicholson at the 1925 Faith Mission Easter Convention entitled:

'The Christian's Peace'

There are two kinds of peace mentioned in the New Testament. The first peace, for blood-washed men and women, is – "Justified by faith, we have peace with God." That is not something that you gain; It is a gift. It is not a payment. The moment you believe, the Lord gives you peace. It does not matter what your denomination may be, or whether you have any denomination, or who you are or what you are, if you are saved by God's grace you have peace with God through our Lord Jesus Christ.

But there is another peace mentioned in Scripture, which you find here in Philippians iv., 7 – "the peace of God, to garrison your heart and mind in Christ Jesus." Every born-again one that has the peace of God, though he should have it. The first peace is determined by your union with the Lord; the second, by your communion with your Lord. If I am walking in the light as He is in the light, we are having fellowship one with another and I possess the peace of God. "Come unto Me... and I will give you rest." This is a first call. But beyond it there is something far richer and deeper. "There remaineth a rest for the people of God," and they who enter into this rest have ceased from their own works, and enter into a possession that is peculiar and wonderfully precious – the peace of God.

........I was once in lodgings where there was only one little boy of six years. One Saturday afternoon he came in saying, "Oh, my head!   I have such a sore head." Before the night was over he was unconscious, and he died of tubercular meningitis. He was their only child. The mother never let him out of her arms. Neighbours offered help, but she held on to the child. When the breath had left the wee body they said, "Give it to us, we will dress it." No, she dressed it herself. When the funeral came, she watched the procession making its way from the door; then she went back to her bed and slept twenty-four hours of unbroken sleep, after which she got up and went back to her work.

Some who did not know any better said, "Tell me, did you love your boy?"
"Does a mother love her only child? Do fish swim? Do birds fly?"

"Why were you not in hysterics like the others? Why did you not cry with inconsolable grief?"

The peace of God, that passeth all understanding, had guarded her heart and mind. I preached for six weeks in that town, but that sermon of hers did more than all the six weeks' preaching.

What did you do when you got into sorrow? What an amount of tearing of hair and hysterics was there! What an amount of dope the doctor had to stick in you! In China they sing and dress themselves in white at a funeral. You and I start to mourn and put black on, and yet they have a heathen religion and we have Christianity.

A friend of mine in Glasgow lived down in Ayrshire, in a beautiful mansion with twenty-five acres round it. He was an out-and out-godly man. One day he was sitting at his breakfast table with the family, reading his correspondence. They had their morning prayer after breakfast, as if nothing had occurred. But, after the children left, he passed a letter to his wife containing the news that every penny they had was gone.

"Well, dear," she said, "we have each other, and, above all, we have CHRIST." They are now in two rooms and kitchen in Glasgow, working for their meat.

Understand it? No, you cannot understand it. In the midst of persecution and opposition, malignity and irritation, one can have this peace. Have you got it? Not only is it incomprehensible in its nature, but it is the peace of a quiet heart. There is no flurry, no tear and wear, no fuss. It is awfully nice to come in contact with people who have a quiet heart. The heart is at rest, with not a flutter or struggle, not a moment's dread or fear of past, present, or future. There is not only a quiet heart, but a quiet conscience, having no fear of God (in the sense of slavish fear) because their sins are buried under the blood. That is the nature of it. The sin question between them and God is settled forever; there is nothing controversial between them and their Saviour.

And it is the peace of a surrendered will. Their delight, day in and day out, is "Not my will, but Thine be done." Jock Troup was singing to us lately of the "sweet beloved will of God." That is mere poetry and sentiment to a whole lot of people; but when you come into this peace you enter into a surrender that is the luxury of life; the delight of the heart. It rejoices you to think that Christ would take the like of you up, it is a glorious place, and a joyful experience, to live day in and day out in God's will.

.........How many are so full of worry, care and anxiety! Take up your Bible and study what God did with worrying people, murmuring people, and you will get a surprise. Whenever you begin to worry or murmur at God, you are charging God's love and will and power. It is a great sin to worry while professing to be in Christ. Thank God, there is a place in Christ where there is "not a shade of worry, not a blast of care," and where all these things are like water on a duck's back. There you have the peace that passeth all understanding, so that you are free to start and serve and help others instead of being merely taken up with your own cares. It is a peace that you cannot understand, but it is also a peace that you cannot misunderstand. Any man or woman who has it will be willing for anything, anywhere.

......What is the source of this peace? "The God of peace be with you always." Seven times in the New Testament you have that expression used about God being the author of peace. You can get peace nowhere else except from Him. There is eternal calm in the Divine Nature: you never get Him worried or flurried. And, just as surely as it is in God, it may be in you and me.

........I knew an old fellow who was hypochondriacal, with more money than sense, and he thought every disease and sickness was coming to him. One day he thought he was dying – and they would have been glad if he had! The doctor advised a trip to the continent, but he came back just as bad as he was. The doctor said to him, - "You want to get out of yourself."

"Man, doctor, how could you get out of yourself?" That's the rub. "The Lord... give you peace by all means." Sister, although your body may be racked with pain and suffering, you can have the peace of God. Although you may be living in a home that is a hell upon earth, with a drunken husband, you can have the peace of God. Although you may be working amongst a most ungodly gang, you can have this peace. And, glory to God, it will be richer the harder your circumstances are. The easier your life and mine is, the less we know about it; but the harder the life is the richer it is. I have learned more on a sickbed than ever I did in a pulpit. I learned more when I was being kicked up and down the country than at any other time. We are wanting to get rid of the trouble, and the Lord says, "I will keep you in the trouble," and He will give you something to glory in while in it.

I remember one of the week-night prayer meetings in an old church in Bangor, at which the late Mr. McLachlan was present after he had lost his wife. A telegram had now come with a message that his boy had been killed in the Boer War; and he stood up in that meeting and said, "Dear friends, I want you to pray for me. Don't pray that I may bear this sorrow, but that I may glory in it." Did you ever get there?

I buried the body of a dear old saint who had walked with her husband on the road to heaven for fifty-six years. When she passed away to meet the Lord the husband said to me, "Mind you, after living and loving during all these years, if it would not be misunderstood, I could shout and praise and magnify God that Maggie's Crowning Day has come; but it might be misunderstood." One Christian widow knelt at the grave of her husband and said, "Blessed Jesus, I thank Thee for fifteen years of heaven on earth."

Yes, it comes "by all means," whether in joy or in sorrow, in tribulation or trial, in poverty or adversity, in work or out of it. It does not matter what your circumstances may be, you have something that will meet your need. Would it not be a testimony for God if every one of us who are saved by His grace would enter into this peace, the peace of God? In the midst of all the varying vicissitudes of life, by all means, this peace comes. It is fine.

Is it some kind of sentimental idea to you? Or it is a real experience in your heart and life? Do you know it? Have you entered into this secret and learned it? Do you possess it amidst all the varieties of experiences, flowing like a river upon your own soul and through your life in benediction and blessing to others?

......Yes! "My peace I give unto you," the Lord said – it is a thing peculiarly His – "I give unto you, not as the world giveth give I unto you." You cannot buy it, you cannot pay any money for it. It is beyond all reckoning. You never merit or deserve it. You may suffer pain or torture in your body, you may give every penny you have to feed the poor, you may go under all kinds of mutilations; but you cannot get peace in that way. God is too big to sell it to you, but He is so big that He gives it. "My peace I give unto you." If you are willing to receive it from Him, to say, "Lord Jesus, I yield me to be Thine, all I have and am I yield to Thee, Lord I receive this blessing – Thy peace, the peace of God that passeth all understanding, to guard and garrison heart and mind," then it is yours.

Mother, you have perhaps felt, as we have talked of these things together, that it has been like peace on earth; but you are going back into a cold world and perhaps a dead church. You feel inclined to say, "My! My! I wish I could stay here and be in this atmosphere; Jesus, let us build three tabernacles up here."

"Oh, no, I want you down there to cast out devils. My peace I give you."

Dear tired mother with aching heart, brother in business, wearied and tired, puzzled and wondering how long this crisis is going to last because you are up against it and full of care, to you Jesus says, "My peace I give, I give, I give." You can have it to-day, and all through the varied experiences of life. And then when it comes to the end of the journey and the end of the day, thank God, that peace that passeth all understanding will garrison the heart and mind.

When I was in the Lanarkshire Christian Union, in Scotland, there was a dear sister called Miss Jack, a long, lanky, stretched-out sort of woman. She did the visiting, and helped a lot. But she was a terror! – a constant rebuke, and a constant inspiration. When she died, it was of tuberculosis, and her body was emaciated, and for days there was hardly a breath in her body. As they sat up with her, it seemed as if every particle of life was gone. They saw her lips moving, and on leaning over her they heard the words:

> *"There's a deep, settled peace in my soul;*
> *There's a deep, settled peace in my soul;*
> *Though the billows of death near me roll,*
> *He abides, CHRIST abides!"*

And so she went in.

Will you go in for this peace – this deeper richer peace, this second rest, this peace of God to garrison your heart and mind?

Lisburn Standard 30th May 1925
REV. W. P. NICHOLSON
To conduct mission at Ballynahinch

Under the auspices of the Ballynahinch and district United Evangelistic Campaign, Rev. W. P. Nicholson will begin a series of meetings at Ballynahinch on Sunday afternoon next. The meetings will be held in a big tent, Church Meadow, and a cordial welcome is extended to all.

Rev. Mr. Nicholson needs no introduction to readers of the "Lisburn Standard," and we learn many converts he made during his rousing campaign in Lisburn are arranging to cross over to Ballynahinch as often as possible to renew old acquaintanceship, and assist in the praise and in every other way they can.

Alliance News
BALLYNAHINCH MISSION

"The year 1924 was also a big year in the history of the Ballynahinch work. In the summer of that year a deputation waited on Rev. W. P. Nicholson, to see if he would consent to conduct a tent mission during June, 1925. This he gladly consented to do, and a large and representative committee from the whole district was formed. Then much prayer began to ascend to God, asking Him to graciously visit the whole district with revival blessing, and there was an abundant answer.

From the very beginning the committee felt that the mission had the Divine approval. The weather was all that could be desired for such a campaign, and the people came crowding in, especially from the country districts. Over 500 persons passed through the enquiry room. These came from a very scattered area, and included two young people from Cork. At the conclusion of the mission a Christian Workers' Union was formed, and the work is being continued on much the same lines.

From: 'Greater Things Than These' by Wm. K. Weir

Many incidents of a deep and serious nature could be retold as memories of that mission. Let us relax for a moment, as we think of a lighter story.

One afternoon during the mission a car drove into the Meadow. An elderly lady, who had never heard Mr. Nicholson and who was anxious to meet him, thinking, mistakenly, as it happens, that there was an afternoon meeting on that day, had asked someone to take her to it in his car. When she discovered her mistake, she decided to wait for the evening meeting. Someone gave her tea and, later on, she was among the crowd when Mr. Nicholson mounted the platform.

The meeting went on and he began to preach. Suddenly, in the middle of the sermon everyone could hear the sound of a car being started up outside. Our poor old friend thought it was the car in which she had come. It was going without her. She would have to leave immediately. But, before she left, she must just shake hands with Mr. Nicholson.

Most people who have interrupted Mr. Nicholson during a sermon have had cause to regret it, but he was surprisingly gentle with this old lady. When she came near him, he seemed at a loss to know what to do, but he accepted her proffered hand and shook it, "Good-bye, Granny," he said, "I'll meet you in heaven."

She appeared to be doubtful about that. "Well," she said, and she paused a good while, "I hope – I hope you'll be there."

The Christian Workers Union Hall at
Windmill Hill, Ballynahinch which was built in 1933

Belfast Telegraph 1st August 1925

MONTH OF NICHOLSON IN BELFAST

Mission in Assembly Hall
During the Whole of August

"Elijah-like herald of the Gospel" was a description recently applied to the Rev. W. P. Nicholson, who is to open a big mission effort in the Assembly Hall, Fisherwick Place, Belfast, on Sabbath afternoon, 2nd August, at 2.30 p.m.

Rev. W. P. Nicholson himself is neither a copy nor an imitation of any present day preacher. His methods are his own, and whatever critics may say in praise or blame, one thing certain is the fact that they appeal to the psychology of the twentieth century. Evidence of the accuracy of this assertion may be found any evening when he is right in the midst of a big campaign, for no building has yet been found which will accommodate all who flock to hear him. It may be admitted that a number on some occasions attend his meetings out of mere curiosity, but the significant thing is that quite a big proportion of those who come to scoff remain to pray. No greater testimony could be given to the success of any evangelist than that, for it means that he fully understands the art of casting "the net on the right side of the ship."

The note he takes up from the Old Testament rings out "My words are unto you men, and my cry is unto the sons of men," and the full trumpet blast from the New Testament is "Come unto me all ye that are weary and heavy-laden."

The Rev. Dr. Montgomery, in a great tribute to Mr. Nicholson, says: "He speaks of sin as the Bible views it; of salvation as the Bible gives it, and of the power from their cruel bondage for ever more. Mr. Nicholson is full of quaint humour, and is a master of racy speech. He has the power of apt illustration, and his gripping and telling words appeal to the crowd in a remarkable way."

"The Christian," a big London religious weekly, states: "There is no reporting device whereby it would be possible to represent in any measure the power that informs Mr. Nicholson's speaking. All the resources of gesture and exclamation, of anecdote and illustration, of colloquialism and badinage and homely denunciation, of humour and tragedy – every conceivable gift – and ability is brought into service and directed to the one single and holy purpose of leading souls to Christ."

During August crowds are sure to verify for themselves these descriptions of the man and his work, which will be conducted throughout the month at the Assembly Hall.

Assembly Hall, Belfast

Belfast Telegraph 3rd August 1925

CROWDED ASSEMBLY HALL

New Nicholson Mission
Faction and Finance Problems

Commercialised Religion "Fashions, Forms, and Follies"

All roads on Sabbath afternoon seemed to lead to the Assembly Hall, Fisherwick Place, Belfast, the scene of the opening meeting in connection with the Nicholson Mission.

The crowds fell under the care of an army of badged and alert ushers in the vestibule. Perhaps nowhere else save in Scotland could the singing have been so wholehearted and so impressive. The surroundings, too, amplified and deepened the spell as one heard rolled out the twenty third Psalm –

> The Lord's my Shepherd; I'll not want,
> He makes me down to lie
> In pastures green; He leadeth me
> The quiet waters by.
>
> My soul He doth restore again
> And me to walk doth make
> Within the paths of righteousness,
> E'en for His own Name's sake.

A glance at the audience quickly revealed that most of the older people had gathered on the ground floor, the younger section having gone to the galleries. There was no cause for surprise in finding that the Psalm all had learned in childhood was being sung with greatest affection and volume by those in the body of the hall. The elder folk immediately in front of the platform took the lead, and most impassioned of all in the rendering was a blind man, who by strange movements of his hands kept the time. What a picture his presence recalled of one similarly afflicted in early Gospel days!

The big assemblage soon changed to another song, breaking forth into an enthusiastic chorusing of "There shall be showers of blessing," followed by a more subdued and reverential rendering of "There's power in the Blood." While the next hymn, "Since Jesus came into my heart," was being sung with great verve, the missioner, the Rev. W. P. Nicholson, arrived, accompanied by the Rev. Dr. Henry Montgomery, the Rev. Thomas Rodgers, the Rev. James Hunter, the Rev. James Tolland, Mr. John King, and Mr. Charles Stewart who as Chairman of the Mission Committee, presided.

The 100th Psalm having been sung, prayer was offered by the Rev. James Tolland, who petitioned for blessing upon the mission by an abundant outpouring of the Holy Spirit and the enthronement of Christ in the hearts of men and women all over the city and in the district to which the influences of the work might extend.

Assembly Hall, Belfast

DR. MONTGOMERY'S FOREWORD

Rev. Dr. Henry Montgomery, introduced by the Chairman as one without whose presence and help no evangelical campaign in Belfast or any other part of the North would be complete, spoke a few words of approval and encouragement. The evangelist, he said, by whose side he stood there, was a life-long friend of his. Both of them belonged to Bangor. Once he used to preach to Mr. Nicholson in Albert Street Church, and at that time his friend was not keen in being near him, jumping over the pews to escape. But thank God those days had gone, and he had the joy now of seeing Mr. Nicholson and himself standing together on the same platform.

The man of Shankhill Road Mission fame, never so appealing, then proceeded to tell why he identified himself with Mr. Nicholson and his work. Smiles provoked by some of his preliminary references to the evangelist, were changed into earnest looks as the vast audience, which packed every part of the building, followed him with closest interest.

"I am here," went on the speaker, in serious tone, "because I still love the Gospel he preaches, and I rejoice infinitely in all God has done by him, and through him, in this part of the world, and indeed in many other parts of the world as well. I am here, also, because I want him to feel once more that although there are multitudes who cannot be here they remember him in prayer and endeavour to support him in his arduous campaign carried on through the holiday season.

"I am here further because I want to commend Mr. Nicholson to you as one who preaches the old Gospel and believes in the Word of God as we understand it. That means that he speaks to men and women of the substitutionary death of Jesus Christ, tells them of a full and free salvation, and lets them know of deliverance from the power of their enemy Satan, and their call to serve God in righteousness and holiness without fear all the days of their lives. It is because Mr. Nicholson preaches all that with such apostolic zeal I am by his side to-day."

The whole house applauded, and Dr. Montgomery went on to tell of the success of Mr. Nicholson as an evangelist both in tent and open-air at the Keswick Convention, fifty coming to the penitent form after one address and going out to win others for the Kingdom. He prayed that God might help and sustain him, making this the best month in the missioner's life.

The Origin of the Mission

In a description of the origin of the mission Mr. Stewart stated that it was first mentioned in a railway carriage. One or two servants of God expressed a wish that Mr. Nicholson might be had for a great campaign in the centre of the city, and the other approved of the suggestion. A worthy elder of the Church, and a well-known Christian worker – these two talked the matter over with others who joined them in praying about it. As a result a committee was formed to take charge of the mission, Mr. Nicholson agreeing to come in August, and a sub-committee approached the Assembly's committee with regard to the use of that building. That committee received them most cordially, and although one or two did not see eye to eye with them the hall was granted. For that act on the part of the Assembly committee they returned thanks, and hoped and believed that at the close of the mission the members would have no cause for regret. It was their conviction that many would be born into the kingdom, and prepared for taking up Christian work in connection with their own churches and congregations.

At this stage Mr. Stewart proceeded to describe to the large assemblage the financial position, after a passing reference to the arrangements. The hall, he said, was costing them £6 a meeting - £12 for the two meetings that day – and there would be extra charges for lighting, advertising, printing, and stationary, which would make up a considerable amount. To meet those charges the committee had decided to take up a collection at each meeting, which would be placed in the hands of the treasurer, who had the assistance of three business men, forming a finance committee. It would therefore be seen that everything was on business lines. If there was any balance over – it might be on the right side or the wrong side – that would be handed over to the evangelist.

Another thing the committee decided – with which Mr. Nicholson had nothing to do – was that at the close of the mission there would be an opportunity for offerings to the missioner. That would be an entirely personal matter between Mr. Nicholson and themselves, the committee would not interfere. They could give just as they were moved to the servant of the Lord who had laboured amongst them. The committee prayed earnestly that God, the Holy Spirit, might descend upon Mr. Nicholson, and open the minds and hearts of all who came to hear him, and that the Lord through His servant would deliver such a message as would set the joybells of Heaven ringing.

By a singular coincidence the Assembly Hall peal of bells broke into a joyous chime, while the audience in emphatic manner, as an accompaniment, expressed their approval of the arrangements made by the committee, financially and otherwise. As a collection was being taken, Mr. Nicholson, addressing the big gathering, said he wanted the whole of it for the C.P.A. in recognition of the help given them by the secretary, Mr. Ewing, and his helpers. So there was cause for a further manifestation of approbation.

After the hymn "There shall be showers of blessing" and prayer, the evangelist delivered his address, taking as his subject "Revival," based on the first eight verses of the eighth chapter of Acts, particularly those describing the wonderful happenings following the preaching of the Gospel and the attendant miracles. At the outset he pointed to the blessings coming as the consequence of revival in the social, business, and industrial situation also in Church life. Emphasising the value of revival, in the Church, he said it would mean the solution of every problem with which she had to deal.

In mentioning a few of these problems, Mr. Nicholson in his own original way referred to the social one. There are individuals, he said, who want to turn the Church into a Sunday self-improvement society, a sort of select and elect place in which an honest man with a ragged suit or a woman of a good heart with a shawl over her head would not feel comfortable. There is this social problem – the problem rich and the poor in the life of the Church – but when men and women come into the House of God every distinction of the kind should be obliterated. The blood of Jesus Christ levels all distinctions, and if the blood of Christ is not allowed to do that the flames of hell would do it –for they make no difference between classes. There is the social problem in the Church; but glory to God, when revival comes it is all wiped out.

"Frozen with Decency"

A second problem, proceeded the speaker, is what people call the "faction or pew problem". There is not a church on earth in which there is not some kind of friction going on at some time. Of course there are churches where no row occurs. A letter came into his hands from a minister to read saying "for any sake don't invite that man into our church. (Laughter.) We have peace here, but bring that man here and my last days will end in strain and storm". There is something worse than a row, remarked the preacher, and it is a false peace. Another – a minister – came up to him and stated, "there is no friction in our church; we are all united". "That is the first time I came across that," he answered. "Oh," said the minister, "we are all frozen together with decency and dignity, and decorum and all the rest of it." But while that is to be found in some churches, went on the speaker, there are scraps in others, and there is nothing for settling them like a blessed revival.

There is another problem said the preacher, with a gesture, and a big one. That is the financial problem. It looks very strange to see the way in which people manage to help God in that respect. They get up a jumble sale – a pair of old trousers, an old dress, old boots. Isn't it pathetic! It makes one blush. When a revival comes all that sort of thing goes out of the back door. "It is desperate the way you commercialise religion", had been remarked to him by a minister. "I was supposed to get £30,000, and I have come back for it," laughingly remarked the preacher, adding, "but I have not got it yet". A comment which made everyone join himself in a smile. His reply was that he would be glad if the man speaking to him would say to his own congregation – as he had done – " I will take just whatever the Lord sends me". But he was told that was a different story. He was not saying a word about getting a salary; but he was showing how he depended upon God for his support. If the Lord did not send a revival he was clean out. There is the financial problem again said the preacher, and when a revival comes all financial needs of the church will be met.

"The Cry from Macedonia"

There is further, declared Mr. Nicholson, the minister and the missionary problem. The cry comes for more missionaries and more ministers. There is a dearth of students, and professors with £1,000 a year are teaching two or three youths. But let a revival come and the men will come, the right class of men – not men with ambiguous experience – there will be ministers and missionaries and Sabbath schoolteachers in abundance.

The civic problem, said the preacher, is another to be solved. Think of the thousands of blood-sucking, publicans in the towns and cities of these countries; then of the many of them in the Church. "I don't know who has a better right to come into a church than the publican," went on the speaker, "but he has no right to be a member of the Church. To be a member he is only eating and drinking damnation to his own soul. A Christian publican! – As well say a Christian harlot! A man in the drink business has the curse of God upon him and his home-breaking damnable traffic".

The preacher, while under this head, charged the Socialism and the Bolshevism abroad in the world to-day against ministers and missionaries who neglected the teaching of the Word of God and taught philosophy instead. That is patent, he stormed, in the case of the Chinese students. To the same neglect is to be traced the deadness of the Church and deserted pews.

The salvation problem, went on Mr. Nicholson, is the next. There is no reason why Jesus planted His Church on earth except for the purpose of solving that problem. Yet how many churches in which there is never registered a conversion! In some the need is denied of any conversion.

The preacher then showed how fashions, forms, and follies take the place of Christ in the Church of today, and dealt with the various hindrances to revival. He asked them to see that revival was not prevented by such things in their lives; but that they asked God to work mightily amongst them as in Pentecostal days by a fresh outpouring of His Spirit.

In the evening Mr. Nicholson again addressed with great power an immense audience in the same building, his subject being "Agents of Revival."

Mr. H. A. Johnston had charge of the praise, and was assisted by a voluntary choir.

The Alliance News

A NEW VENTURE WITH GREAT POSSIBILITIES IN IT
Preparing the way for an Alliance Bible School

There are many reasons for which the Nicholson Mission, held in Belfast during the month of August, will ever live in the memory of many of God's people. Of these, however, perhaps none of them will serve more to perpetuate the memory of the mission than the attempt, which was made at the close of the mission, to form a Bible School in Belfast. At the final meetings of the mission it was announced that such a step was about to be made. The announcement met with a most hearty response, and immediately the names of scores of young men, interested in the movement, began to pour in.

The first meeting of the new undertaking was held on Monday, 31st August, when the Minor Hall of the Y.M.C.A., Wellington Place, was crowded with a band of keen, enthusiastic men, young and old. At this meeting the nature of the proposed classes was explained and an interesting talk given on the subject by the Rev. James Hunter, M.A.

The Bible School at Magdalene Hall Men's Class

The Belfast Telegraph 1925

"No Slicing up of the Bible"
New School for Belfast
Inaugural Meeting in Y.M.C.A.

The new Bible Study School formed at the Magdalene Hall, Shaftesbury Square, Belfast, under the auspices of the Irish Alliance of Christian Workers' Unions, was inaugurated at a large public meeting in the Y.M.C.A. Hall, Wellington Place, on Friday evening, when a most impressive address was delivered by Rev. W. P. Nicholson.

Prior to these proceedings the students, numbering about 200 or more, with warm friends of the movement, were entertained to tea in the Cafe Royal adjoining. When the gathering was over a large band of young men left the building singing "Away over Jordan we'll wear a crown," and marched through Donegall Place, Royal Avenue, and other main thoroughfares.

Prayer having been offered by Rev. John Ross.

The President of the Alliance, Mr. Harry Walker, Kirkcubbin, said that meeting was proof that the Word of God was still the power of God unto salvation. The fact had been forced upon them that in order to preserve the things that belonged to them as the redeemed of God they must have a Christian Workers' Alliance which would welcome every brother and sister in the Lord irrespective of class or creed or nationality. They stood for the whole Bible, and not a mutilated one. Hence it was absolutely necessary that there should be a linking up of their various Unions, and that there should be connected with that work men who would be the means of holding them all together. They further believed that the missionaries sent forth to other lands should be men and women who proclaimed the Word of God faithfully and truly, and for that reason they asked for the support of all who believed in the Book of books.

Mr. James Mairs, Donaghadee, said they were not going to emphasise their denominational differences, but to emphasise the work in which all were engaged. The time was when if a man got converted any one who took him to a particular Church was accused of proselytism. This had convinced them of the need for a Christian Workers Alliance, which enabled people to join together for a common work. Did anyone say they were out against the Church, which might be taken as a perversion of the truth – something from the devil? The value of the Bible was then pointed to by the speaker, who said they were not going to have any slicing up of the Divine Word. They were not out to form a new Church, but they were going to see that the Churches already existing would stick to the things they professed. (Applause.)

Succession of the Prophets

Rev. James Hunter, speaking of the help received from the Scriptures when diligently studied, said the world accounted them as dirt, and it was just them that the Holy Spirit through them was working wonders. They were in the succession of the prophets. To come after Christ they were to be in revolt against everything that was opposed to the truth. They had also got to believe the Bible was not man's word, but God's Word.

The devil did not say the Bible was not God's Word, but he told them to misuse its contents. The whole purpose of the Bible School was to let the lion loose: the Word of God would be its own defence. They were there to affirm the Word of God and the power of God, and in that faith to propagate the Word of God they were prepared to go to the ends of the earth. The Word of God transformed homes; and more than that, it transformed themselves. (Applause.)

Rev. W P. Nicholson said they had been meeting here and there, but now they had got their own meeting place – the old Magdalene Hall. It was delightful to see so many gathered there to give the school a start. They hoped before long to have their own Bible Training School, so that it would not be necessary to send their workers to Glasgow for preparation. (Applause) The young men would have their nights in the new Bible School and the young women would have their nights also. Eventually they would be sending out men and women for mission work at home and in the regions beyond.

There were many, continued the speaker, who could not tell truth from error. But they were determined to stand by all the old ways. It made him mad when he read of the Covenanters and looked at some of the "warts" who were trying to upset their work from the inside. Luther used to say before he went into one of his great contests, "O Lord, I am not cowardly, but strengthen me in the work I have to do". That was also their prayer, and in the spirit of it they determined to go forth to battle for the truth.

In the remainder of his address, the speaker showed how the Bible had withstood all attacks made upon it, and said they were called upon to defend it not only with their talents, but also with their lives.

There were also on the platform Rev. Samuel Simms, James Toland, Wilbur Pyper, W. J. Harrison, Messrs. Charles Stewart, Archibald Irwin, J.P., George Hopper, John King, George Lynn, R. G. Bass, A. Graham, J. Apperson (Hon. Treasurer), J. A. Ross, B.A. (Hon. Secretary); A. Kerr, M. Nesbitt, H. H. Palmer, E. Wightman, T. H. Watson and W. J. Hill.

The meeting concluded with the benediction.

The Northern Whig– December 1925

The Faith Mission Christmas Conferences were continued on Saturday in the Y.M.C.A. Hall, Wellington Place. The meetings, which were held in the forenoon and afternoon, were very largely attended. At the former Mr. J. B. McLean presided, and an address was given by Rev. W. P. Nicholson.

Mr. Nicholson said his subject had to do with pre-Pentecostal and post-Pentecostal belief and the case of a man or woman who thought Pentecost merely an historical thing. Some people seemed disposed to believe themselves saved, but absolved from living an out-and-out Christian life. They said they would live what they regarded as a normal life. They had that choice, but they could not avoid its consequences. They could, if they liked, live a pre-Pentecostal experience, but there would be certain results.

In the first place they would be in doubt whether they were saved or not. To anybody asking – "Are you saved?" their reply would be – "I hope, I trust, I believe, I think I am! And not "I am sure and certain that I am." That was the normal condition and experience of a man and woman who was living a pre-Pentecostal experience, a man or woman who had never gone from Calvary to Pentecost.

"Supposing someone asked me," said the preacher, "Nicholson, are you married?"

"Imagine me replying," said Mr. Nicholson – "I hope I am." I am as dead sure I am as I am confident of being in the Y.M.C.A. at this moment. Until you are endued with the post-Pentecostal experience you will never have anything but bewilderment and wondering whether you are truly and actually born again or not.

Exterior view of Y.M.C.A., Wellington Place

Why, he asked, should they live that kind of life? If they were truly born again! They did not enjoy the old life. They might go back, but there would be nobody as miserable and wretched. Unless they had this post-Pentecostal experience they would always have unsettled views about the various things concerning their life and mind. They would never get to the point where they could say, "The Word of God says it, and I believe it! How many men and women had unsettled views about salvation? The idea they had about salvation was a most pathetic thing. They were carried away by one wind of doctrine after another, and were not grounded firmly in the Truth of Christ. They were "bairns and children" instead of matured men and women!

The same thing applied about the Bible. The Bible to such was a sealed book. It did not open its Truth to them, and they had unsettled views about the coming of Christ, but they learned more about the fundamentals of faith and mind in the teaching of the Holy Ghost than they ever would from the wisest professor. If they made up their minds to have a pre-Pentecostal experience in post-Pentecostal days they would have a good reputation in some quarters. Some would say, "That is the kind of Christian I like. That rough-tongued ignorant, coarse fellow, Nicholson, hammering and slammering and battering at folks, I can't follow at all." (Laughter) Others who would share in this good reputation to which he referred were the minister's wife who led in the Sunday School dances and the chap who was praised as "a good mixer, you know, and none of your fanatics or dictating sort of creatures."

"The Worldly Church"

A minister had written to him, he added, laying down a lot of stipulations as to what he was to say and how to say it, and his reply to him was that if he came to his church under such conditions he would be nothing more than tinkling cymbals and sounding brass. He thanked God that he was a sworn enemy to every enemy of Jesus Christ. When the worldly church began to speak well of them their power was doomed. He remembered on one occasion hearing the late General Booth address a meeting. At the time he was surrounded by many people in exalted positions and by dignitaries, and he said: - "Fellow soldiers, I am trembling today for the safety of the Salvation Army. While they were vilifying and cursing us we had the power of God and the smile of God, but since all these dignitaries have been smiling on me I am trembling for the 'ould' Army". So he (Mr. Nicholson) began to tremble when certain classes of people said he was a good fellow. It was a sad thing to see a lot of "born-again" men and women having favour with an unsanctified and half-saved crowd. They would have a good reputation amongst carnal Christians if they made up their minds not to go in for the experience of which he was speaking. They would be terribly scared about "fanaticism", and hear talk about "emotionalism", and "sensationalism", and revivals, and about working upon the feelings of the people. When they heard some of those poor ministers, with all their psychological knowledge, they knew just exactly where they were, but there was nothing more emotional than salvation. Could they have "love, joy, peace," without feeling emotion? Imagine one saying he had joy but did not feel happy, and putting on a face like a Lurgan peat spade. "Oh," someone would severely inform them, "I believe in an unemotional, intellectual religion, you know. But these wild fireworks. Hallelujahs and glories to God. Oh, no." The professions of a man so wholly without fervour never could be pleasing to the Deity. If that was their attitude of mind they would stumble at believers, and would say that such people were crazy and drunk – full of new wine. "No," St. Peter would say, "it is only nine o'clock and the pubs are not open." (Laughter.) Let them go into some of their church services and, continued Mr. Nicholson, "Could you imagine them drunk – drunk with religion? Could you? Man, they are as sober as a corpse." (Laughter) He had, he said, been preaching at Bangor, where he had been born and raised, and where he was well known. An elder in one of the churches said: "I have been forty years an elder of this church, and this is the first time I have ever seen a minister laugh in that pulpit." Did they think because they were ministers they could not laugh, and was that why they put black coats and night shirts on them?

If they had made up their minds not to go in for the post-Pentecostal experience they would become a reproach to Christ and bring shame upon His name, and disgrace and dishonour upon His Church. If that was the kind of experience they had been living they need not continue it. Christ could free them from all that nonsense and rubbish, and they could abandon themselves to His love.

1926

Alliance News – January 1926

THE IRISH ALLIANCE OF CHRISTIAN WORKERS' UNIONS
Its Origin and Aims by T. Bailie (Bangor)

Within the space of another three or four months, this organization will have been two years in existence. If ever a movement had its birthplace amid the counsels of God, assuredly such applies to the work above mentioned. For a considerable number of years past there had been springing up, here and there in various parts of the Northern Province, small communities of the Lord's people, belonging to various churches and denominations, whose desire was to unite together in aggressive gospel effort. Probably the oldest of these earlier organizations was the one known as the "Bangor Christian Workers' Society," the formation of which about half a century ago was largely due to Dr. Henry Montgomery (now of Shankhill Road Mission, Belfast) and his brother, Mr. S. T. Montgomery, who has faithfully and devotedly carried on the work to the present day.

In addition to the Bangor society, other similar organizations came into being at occasional intervals. Not, however, until the beginning of the Rev. W. P. Nicholson's work in this country over five years ago can it be said that the formation of Christian Workers' Unions, on the lines of those which exist today, made any distinct advance in point of numbers.

As a result, however, of the widespread blessing experienced through the ministry of the evangelist referred to, and incidentally, of the work of others of the Lord's servants, there has been a steady increase in the number of organizations thus formed over various parts of the country. All these Unions were isolated and independent of each other, and in many cases unknown to one another. It was this condition of things which caused the desire to arise in the hearts of a number of God's people situated widely apart, that some means might be found to unite and solidify in one homogeneous whole the many Unions then formed.

Thus it happened in the Providence of God that the workers in Derry, Belfast, Ards, and Portadown found themselves simultaneously in communication with one another on the same subject and with the same desire.

Following a preliminary conference in Derry on Boxing Day, 1923, a larger conference was convened in Belfast, 1924, and there the organization now known as The Irish Alliance of Christian Workers' Unions received its first impetus. For over a year the work has been carried on under purely honorary control, and progress has been of necessity slower than would otherwise have been the case.

Despite this disadvantage, however, it is a matter of much thankfulness to be able to record that already over thirty Unions have been formed and others are in process of formation. The work of consolidating these Unions and placing the movement upon a soundly organized basis has been a matter of serious concern to the Council, the embers of which have given themselves whole-heartedly to the interests of the Alliance, and in consequence the decision to appoint a full-time organizer was unanimously agreed upon some months ago.

After much prayerful consideration, the council were led to the appointment of Mr. J. Allen Ross, B.A., upon whose shoulders now rest the responsibilities of organization and control. Mr. Ross brings to the work all the advantages of earnest and consecrated zeal and an amount of undoubted talent and ability that augurs well for the future of the movement. The earnest prayers of every reader are solicited that his ministry as leader and organizer of this important work for God may be abundantly blessed.

The objects of the Alliance are by this time, we trust, sufficiently well known to render repetition unnecessary. Briefly may it be stated that while the Alliance is strictly non-sectarian, it is wholly interdenominational. It is not opposed to, but is intended to be a complement to, the existing work of the Churches. An important condition of membership to a Christian Workers' Union is that members must also be members of a recognized evangelical Church.

The primary object of a Christian Workers' Union is to provide a common platform upon which all believers may unite in whole-hearted and aggressive effort for Christ, irrespective of denominational distinctions or differences. Surely in this modernistic age, when violent assaults are being made upon the evangelical position and when, sometimes from unexpected quarters, we hear taunts and jibes at what is derisively termed "the old-fashioned traditionalism," it is incumbent upon God's people to sink denominational differences and join together in defence of the faith. Whilst it is true that the enemy has been seeking to sow the seeds of division and discord amongst the saints of God, we are nevertheless able to rejoice that thus far so many have stood true to the cause of Christian unity and to the Master's ideal, to which He gave expression when He said "That they may be one."

This then, briefly, is the aim of the Alliance, not to divide, but to unite; to sow the seed, not of discord, but of Christian love; to bring together in the bonds of Christian love and fellowship and in aggressive whole-hearted endeavour those who desire to follow Him in lowly-hearted and consecrated service.

What then shall be the motto of the Alliance for 1926? Shall it not be "One in Christ"! If so, may we urge you to help to make it practical by assisting, as far as you can, in the work of the Alliance. Become a member of your local Christian Workers' Union. If none is yet formed in your district, get in touch with the organizing secretary, who will set the matter going. Above all, join us in earnest believing prayer that work of consolidating the movement may be abundantly blessed and that the result may be showers of blessing to and then through a United Church of God.

Alliance News – 1926
(Re: Christian Workers Union)

THE WORK IN AND AROUND LONDONDERRY

On Easter Sunday, 1922, that much-hated and much-loved servant of the Lord, Rev. W. P. Nicholson, started in Londonderry the great campaign which, through the power of the Holy Spirit, resulted in the salvation of hundreds of precious souls, and also in the formation of the Derry C.W.U.

We can well remember the inaugurating of the Union in Carlisle Road Methodist Church. It was a beautiful evening in May, and at the close of the meeting, marshalled by Mr. R. G. Bass, of the I.E.S., about three hundred were led forth in the first open-air march, in which many reputations died, the funerals taking place the following evening.

Since its inception the Lord has set His seal on the work of the Union in a wonderful way, many precious souls having been saved through its agency.

We are looking forward with real expectancy to the visit of our beloved brother, Rev. W. P. Nicholson, to our city during January (1926), and we ask all our friends to unite with us at the Throne of Grace for a real devil-defeating, soul-saving time.

A donkey and cart bearing Good News.
The donkey is inside the box-like structure

Derry Sentinel 5th January 1926

REV. W. P. NICHOLSON IN DERRY
"Etiquette and Decorum of the Pulpit"

Londonderry Guildhall was packed to overflowing on Sunday night when Rev. W. P. Nicholson opened a month's evangelistic mission in the city. When every seat in the hall was filled there still remained some hundreds on the stairs and in the landing, and the struggle to get inside only ceased when Mr. Nicholson himself begged the ushers to take no more trouble with chairs, as it was impossible to get any more people seated.

Later some outside the doors were causing considerable liveliness when Mr. Nicholson addressing them, said, "It is not our fault if you cannot get in, but you are not going to spoil the comfort of hundreds inside. I am not like some preachers who have their eyes on their manuscript all the time. I can see all around me. I can see exactly how you are taking your medicine, and if I notice anybody not behaving himself, God help him."

Further on in the meeting Mr. Nicholson had again to admonish a number of people on the stairs. "We are not going to have this service disturbed," he said, "and we will clear those stairs if you do not behave yourselves. Remember, you cannot disturb a public meeting. You are not in a Sinn Fein country here; mind that. We are not going to be disturbed by a bunch of 'hoboes' in this hall. Some of you men go out to those people there, or will I go myself? I never saw one of you that I could not lick" he told the noisy group. "If you don't want to come to the meeting, you can stay away, but if you come you will do as you are told."

It was like coming home again, Mr. Nicholson said, to arrive back in Derry Guildhall. They hoped to have glorious experiences together during the coming month. "Some sort of renegade preacher down in Armagh has said that the efforts of these missions wither away in a night," he remarked, "but if that man came to this part of the country he would not say that." Some people thought that the etiquette and decorum of the pulpit meant everything but, glory to God, he was not one of those. "The devil is not pleased with this mission," he declared, "and every blood-sucking God-cursed publican is against it, as well as every 'ould' brewer or distiller."

Later Mr. Nicholson sympathised with the women who were unable to find seats. "At the end of the hymn," he remarked, "some of you young fellows who have seats might give them to the girls. You never know what might happen out of it," he added, amidst a burst of laughter. He recalled that he made a similar request in Belfast some time ago, and had given a similar hint as to what might result from it, "and do you know," he added, to the accompaniment of another ripple of laughter. "The other day I got a letter in Dublin from a young man, saying – "Dear sir, it happened that night." "So you never know where a blister may rise," he commented, while the audience enjoyed another laugh.

"What is a Christian?"

Dealing with the subject, "What is a Christian?" Mr. Nicholson said – A Christian was a man who believed the Bible was the infallible Word of God. He believed the Bible not only contained the Word of God but that it actually was the Word of God. Anyone who did not believe in the infallibility of the Book, if he was an honest man, might call himself a Unitarian, or a Roman Catholic, or anything else he liked, but he had no right to the name of Christian.

That Book declared there was a heaven and a hell, the one as sure and as everlasting as the other. Many men denied what Christianity stood for, yet wanted to hold on to the name of Christian. If they had the same honesty amongst their professors and ministers, as they had amongst their politicians, it would be a good thing for the Church. If a politician lost faith in his party he would resign, despite the loss of a lucrative position. "Would it not be a grand thing," he asked, if those men and women in our churches, pulpits and colleges today who have lost faith in the Word of God would say so and resign? They would get the esteem and respect as well as the sympathy of every genuine Christian, but, while they stick to their fat salaries and soft jobs and seek to wreck the very thing they should preach, they are beneath our respect."

No one, he added, who denied the Virgin birth or the Immaculate Conception could be a Christian. He took off his hat to the Roman Catholic faith in that respect. While he held no brief for that faith, which, he thought, was degenerating, yet he must say Roman Catholics spoke well of Mary, and they spoke well of Jesus, and they upheld the Immaculate Conception.

A writer in an American magazine had tried to show that Jesus' blood was no more effective than the blood of goats or bulls, but that it was only His obedience to God and His life that counted.

"He is a liar, like his father the devil, and a double-barrelled one at that," Mr. Nicholson declared. If they denied the Resurrection or began to allegorise it, they could not be called by the name of Christian. A Christian must also believe that all had sinned and that everyone was born corrupt.

Evolution, the preacher continued, told them that man was going upward and onward and that Jesus Christ was only the outcome of evolutionary progress. "If you believe that, call yourselves by any name you like, but don't say you are Christians," he advised his audience. To talk of Christian evolution was to talk of a virtuous harlot. The terms were mutually antagonistic. Salvation was only obtainable through believing in Christ as the personal Saviour. The best-living man or woman in the world who did not believe in Christ would be damned in hell. The surest road to hell they could take was to believe that if they lived a good life, attended their church regularly, and paid their dues, God would forgive them for Christ's sake.

If they were real Christians, there must be no secret about it. He understood that members of societies, such as the Freemasons and the Orangemen, were pledged to secrecy. It must be a terrible oath they take, because, when he was young, he was one of a party who half-drowned a big Mason when speechless drunk to try to get some secrets out of him. Drunk as he was, he would tell them not a word, although they "doused" him often. If they were pledged to secrecy when they became a Freemason or an Orangeman they were pledged to publicity when they became Christians. They must tell it and try to get others to join them. No genuine Christian could make a secret out of his Christianity.

Rev. Mr. Nicholson, on his arrival in Londonderry on Saturday, was received by the committee and executive of the Christian Workers' Union and entertained at afternoon tea in Stevenson's. About fifty people were present.

The Guildhall, Londonderry
Where the Rev. W. P. Nicholson's Mission was conducted

Alliance News – 1926
LONDONDERRY
Report

We in Derry saw wonderful times during January, when we had a return visit from the Rev. W. P. Nicholson. Four years have gone since he conducted his last (or his first) mission in Derry, and Mr. Nicholson's heart must have warmed as he saw the four-year-old converts working in the enquiry rooms and elsewhere. Surely these young men and women are "living epistles, known and read of all men."

From the human point of view the mission was handicapped, the meetings unavoidably alternating between the Guildhall and Ebrington Presbyterian Church. But is there anything too hard for the Lord? In spite of the scene shifting, every night found a packed building and a deepening interest. In fact, the whole city was moved, and Mr. Nicholson and the mission proved fruitful sources of conversation during his stay in Derry. Most unlikely people turned up night after night, and many of them were to be seen among the crowd of anxious souls streaming to the enquiry rooms.

It was a wonderful time which we shall never forget, and our prayers and good wishes follow Mr. and Mrs. Nicholson on their journey to Australia.

PORTADOWN
Much Blessing at Portadown
An example in steadfastness and courage

Our thanks are due to God for the work that is going on at Portadown. The following, being extracts from reports dealing with the various aspects of the work, reveal to us the progress made and the blessing enjoyed.

"In presenting the report of our fourth year's work, the committee desires to thank God for all the blessings and guidance received, not only during the past year, but also from the very commencement of our Union. God's blessing has so signally rested upon us that we believe no spiritual work outside the Churches has, during recent years, been so much blessed in Portadown. Our membership is increasing in numbers, and deepening in spirituality, and not only taking their full share in the aggressive work of their own individual churches, but are spreading the light in churches, halls, and open-air, and helping individually and by deputation to other Unions over a wide area in Ulster. Further, the loyalty of our members to the Saturday night open-air meetings is a cause of thankfulness, and also the crowds that stand patiently listening to the testimonies and songs of the brothers and sisters who confess their Lord and praise Him for His saving and keeping power. Eternity alone will reveal the good work done at our open-air meetings.

"We believe one of the reasons for the success of our Union is that it stands for a whole Bible from cover to cover. It believes in the inspiration and inerrancy of God's Word, in the Sovereignty of God, in the Virgin Birth and Deity of the Lord Jesus, and in the Personality of the Holy Spirit. Three in One and One in three, in the Fall of Man, in the Ruin by Sin, in Redemption by the Blood, and in Regeneration by the Holy Spirit.

"Four years ago the Rev. W. P. Nicholson held a great mission at Portadown, as a result the Christian Workers' Union was established. A yearning desire to see greater things for God led the members to consider the advisability of inviting this Ulster evangelist to hold another united mission. Many obstacles that to man seemed well-nigh impossible to surmount presented themselves, but believing that if it was in God's will that this mission should be held He would remove difficulties, and open up the way, led members to fresh intercession and prayer to God, to make known His will concerning their desire.

Interior of "Mary Street Cathedral" Portadown (1926)

"Owing to various causes none of the churches were available. An offer of what was once a potato store was made. It had a clay floor, walls were black and forbidding, and no seating accommodation. It was decided to make the most of this offer, and it is wonderful how things began to brighten. A cement floor was laid, and one of the members offered to seat the hall at a nominal sum on condition that free labour was provided. To-day it is known as Mary Street Cathedral, and large audiences listened night after night to clear, forcible Gospel addresses, and saints have been edified and souls saved. The audiences have been so large that no other building in the town would have held them, proving once again that the Gospel is still the power of God to attract and hold men and women. Looking back over the mission, we find it impossible to express our thankfulness to God for His goodness and grace, and we can only exclaim:' How marvellous! How wonderful!"

News Letter – 23rd March 1926

CHRISTIAN WORKERS' UNION
Success of Rev. W. P. Nicholson's Mission

Representatives of the Christian Workers' Union from all parts of Ulster were present at Ravenhill Presbyterian Church, Belfast, last night to bid farewell to the Rev. W. P. Nicholson, the well-known evangelist, and Mrs. Nicholson, who are leaving shortly for Australia and New Zealand, after which they will continue their work in South Africa.

Charabancs and motor buses brought contingents of people from Portadown, Lurgan, Banbridge, Bangor, Ballynahinch and other centres, with the result that the church was crowded an hour before the proceedings were due to commence. The meeting was under the auspices of the committee of the mission conducted in the Assembly Hall last August and the Alliance of Christian Workers Unions.

Mr. Charles Stewart, who presided, said they thanked God for the soul-stirring times they had in the revival movement of the last five years. Only eternity would reveal the vast multitude of souls won for Christ during that period. There was scarcely an evangelical Protestant congregation in Ulster that was not spiritually richer and stronger for the blessing received. They were all exceedingly sorry at the thought of parting with their dear friends, Mr. and Mrs. Nicholson, whose messages had been so fruitful in results.

Rev. W. P. Nicholson said it was with mingled feelings that they met on such an occasion as that. He wished them the very best that God could give them and the very best that God could make them. God was not a pacifist. He was a God of war and of battle, and he (the speaker) did not know of any religion that should appeal more strongly to Irishmen than the religion of the Lord Jesus Christ. It would take all the red blood in them. Mr. Nicholson went on to say that everything he had he owed to the Christian Workers' Union. In the halls around Bangor he got splendid training for the work in which he had been engaged for well nigh 26 years. If their work was to be carried on, sane organisation had to be started, and he knew none better than the Christian Workers' Union. There were branches in North, South and East Belfast, and to be a member they had also to be a member of their own Church. It was not against the Churches. He must say that some of their ministers were not evangelical in their efforts. He would like to warn people against becoming entangled with ceremonial. They were not making light of the Sacrament, but they must not get entangled with it. People made too much of things that God made mighty little of. They must stand in their liberty, but that did not mean lawlessness. They must live in a law of love. He deplored the teaching that much of the Bible was allegorical and traditional. The Message of God went to their hearts, and told men to stand firm – to stand firm in the faith.

Rev. Samuel Simms, presiding at an overflow meeting in the lecture hall, said the best answer they could make to critics of Mr. Nicholson was to live the life of faith. The churches in Ulster where their brethren had received Mr. Nicholson were showing increased prosperity and increased congregations, while others were in a very different position.

In the course of the evening Mr. and Mrs. Nicholson were presented with a cheque. Mrs. Nicholson also received a gold wristlet watch, and friends from Ballynahinch presented Mr. Nicholson with two rugs.

The Alliance News – April 1926

THE REV. W. P. NICHOLSON AT CAMBRIDGE
A University Stirred

"There was a man sent from God whose name was William P. Nicholson." That is what men and women by the score are saying in Cambridge today, now that the Mission to the University is over.

It is an established custom to hold a Mission to the students in Cambridge every three years. The Lent Term is chosen, and usually three men of varying outlook and religious experience are invited as Missioners. This year the Bishop of Manchester, Dr. F. W. Norwood, of the City Temple, and Dr. Stuart Holden were the men asked to give God's message to the University from 30th January to 7th February. Mr. Nicholson was invited to conduct some meetings in anticipation of Dr. Holden's visit, and arrived in Cambridge on Tuesday, 26th January, only to find that his friend Dr. Holden had just been forbidden by his doctor to fulfil the engagement for the following week.

At once there came an invitation from the Mission Committee to Mr. Nicholson, who consented to fill the place thus left empty at the last moment.

There were some who had misgivings. W. P. Nicholson is no ordinary man – and he is not without his traducers as well as his critics! But the Cambridge Inter-Collegiate Christian Union – a band of earnest and aggressive undergraduates rallied round him to a man, and Mr. Nicholson, after confessing that he never would have left Ireland had he known what was in store for him, threw himself heart and soul into the work.

It was a cause of wonderment to many why it was that night after night the audiences increased and the interest deepened. For Mr. Nicholson is admittedly no scholar, in the University sense of the term; neither is he careful to garb his message in the smooth conventionalities of many modern pulpits. Swift, straight, and direct are his blows, and many a man winced under his stinging and caustic utterances. He sweeps aside shams, and by studied exaggeration lays bare the excuses and the sins that keep men from God.

And the results? Night by night men turned to God in repentance and faith. An audience of undergraduates is not an easy one to handle, but by his geniality, no less than by his searching and arresting messages, Mr. Nicholson won the hearts of his hearers, not only to himself, but to the Lord, whose Word he so faithfully proclaimed.

A host of Cambridge friends will follow God's servant in prayer and remembrance as he sails shortly for the Antipodes, and will thank God that ever they were brought into touch with William P. Nicholson.

IMPRESSIONS OF NICHOLSON
by Dublin Rector -1926

The following is an article which appeared in the "Church of Ireland Gazette" from the pen of Rev. T. Hammond, Dublin.

Many years ago now trouble broke out at the docks in Cork. It was resolved by the Shipping Federation that the strike should be broken. Accordingly a gang of strike-breakers was imported. Weedy wasters from Cockneyland for the most part. Mingling among them here and there a daredevil with iron in his blood and madness in his brain. They were berthed in a vessel anchored in mid-stream and convoyed there and back under a heavy guard. Those were the days when the sardonic humour of economics classed clerks with capitalists – hence this inside knowledge.

Irish dockers, like Defoe, had a short way with dissenters, which might easily become "the shortest way." To avoid, so the papers said, unnecessary recriminations, the public houses were picketed. There was prohibition, except on the river, for the strike breaker. Most of the champions of freedom had an unholy thirst. One of them tumbled aboard greatly aggrieved, and after the manner of his kind grumbled aloud to nobody in particular. "'Ere," he says, with extended hands, "Wot kind er a ploice is this 'ere. I gowes for a glass of beer, an' a bloke 'e says ye cawnt go in there, 'e says. Wy, I says. Because ye cawnt, 'e says. 'E was a bloke with a hulster awn. Oo is 'e, eny 'ow?" A tired voice from a neighbouring bunk called out: "I'll tell ye, moite. E 's a retired Sunny school teacher, that's wot 'e is."

No one ever called Nicholson that. Nicholson has achieved fame. Moody, Spurgeon, and now Nicholson have been pilloried in the public press. The "unco guid" have gnashed their teeth and Boreas has come out with a snorting nor'easter. "He is course, he is vulgar, he is awful!" Most of his critics have never heard him. None of them know him. Will the "Gazette" permit me to present another side of the question? Nicholson has power. Watch his audience when he gets in the strike of a great subject. See the rapid alternations as the flitting emotions find expression in their faces. Now the laugh that so jars the funerally respectable. Now the strained expectancy as he leads them step by step in thought to a fitting d'enouement. Again the soft sigh of released tension when a period of dramatic vividness comes to a close. This is no idle buffoonery. Here at all events is a man who out of the well of human experience draws deep draughts. It will surprise and astonish the critics, but we believe that Nicholson is full of the Holy Ghost. The modern pulpit manipulator leaves these things in the Acts of the Apostles. They furnish appropriate sermons for Whit Sunday, but must not be overstrained. But there are some who look for spiritual power today and get it. Nicholson has got it.

"But he is vulgar." So was Elijah when he taunted the prophets of Baal. So was Ezekiel when he rebuked the Israel of his day. His picture of a neglected child is not set for a drawing room. Prophets are men of direct speech. Nicholson has gone down into the depths. He knows the strange stirrings of primitive emotions. And he speaks the language of the man he wants to reach. Ordinary clergymen live in a world of faint "damns," and seem to forget that there are men in their congregations who call them "padre" since the war, and who have privately a vocabulary that is sufficiently lurid for all practical purposes. The talk of the smoke-room is hushed when the black shadow of a priest darkens the door; and, poor fool, he thinks the men he knows with their occasional oath and quick apology, represents the men that are. Nicholson knows differently, and the foul-mouthed church-goers rail at him because he knows and lets them know. It is not pleasant work, but it is necessary, and hence the man. If we told our people the truth perhaps our churches would empty of some smooth-faced hypocrites, but perhaps also the sinner would come in. At present "the man in the street" remains in the street.

And look at the graphic power behind the realism of the man. We have companied with him under a tropical moon in the shades of an African forest as he paced to and fro crying "O God, if I could forget!" We have sat with the nameless and homeless men of the mining camp who sobbed as if their heart would break because a mulatto girl sang "Your mother is still praying for you, Jack." We have seen the storm gather on the mountain and the little burn that kissed the land into fertility suddenly transformed into a raging torrent. We have heard the grinding of the brakes as the night express came to a sudden pause before the broken bridge, and the wild cry of the Highland lad who flung himself before it that, by his life, he might bring that pause and save the sleeping passengers. Then we have gazed with a new and reverential awe on the thorn-crowned Sufferer. Who went to death for us. The man who can make earth and air and sea speak to us of the undying love of Calvary has something beside vulgarity. He knows men, but in the sublime moments of his great speeches he persuades men that he knows God.

And it is a libel fashioned by the devil himself to say that this man is indifferent to righteousness. We have knelt with scores of others while we repeat it –

> **"I take the promised Holy Ghost,**
> **I take the gift of Pentecost,**
> **To fill me to the utmost.**
> **I take – He undertakes."**

We have the heart-searching concerning restitution, forgiveness, witness, service, and never once the flag lowered. Never once was the gate opened to admit a single enemy of right, truth, and love. With passionate pleading this man who had been snatched as a brand from the burning, begged us, entreating even with tears, that God and God only should be all and all in our lives. And there have been gracious answers in Christians possessed with a new vitality, who will yet render signal service to the Most High.

And he scorches and blisters and sears the smug hypocrites. He withers with scorn the brain-proud word-spinners. He lets his fierce indignation burn against the problem-setters who speculate on a fallen humanity and leave the souls they have psychologised to perish.

And ever there rises to his lips the great cry: "O God! May we never grow used to hearing the thud of Christless feet on the road to hell."

From: W.P. NICHOLSON
Flame for God in Ulster by S.W. Murray

DEATH OF MRS. NICHOLSON

Mr. Nicholson began a series of campaigns in Sydney, Australia, in June 1926. While in Australia, Mrs. Nicholson died suddenly during one of the missions. He continued holding campaigns in various cities and towns but eventually he was obliged to cancel the remainder of his Australian tour on account of illness, and he had to take six months complete rest on medical advice.

While in Australia he married Fanny Elizabeth Collett and subsequently returned to his home in Los Angeles, California. Mrs. Nicholson's care and support in the work meant much to her husband in the following years, in which they travelled to take part in evangelistic missions in various parts of the world.

1928

Belfast Telegraph 27th September 1928

WELCOME TO REV. W. P. NICHOLSON

Rev. W. P. Nicholson, the well-known evangelist who is a native of Bangor, was given a cordial welcome by a crowded audience in the King's Hall, Bangor, on Wednesday evening on the commencement of a week's mission in Bangor, to be followed by a campaign in Glasgow.

Mr. Nicholson is a son of the late Captain John Nicholson of Bangor, and his mother and sister were present on the platform. A hearty welcome was also extended to the evangelist's wife, who expressed her pleasure at being in her husband's home town.

Tea was provided, and afterwards Mr. S. G. Montgomery, President of the Bangor Christian Workers' Society, occupied the Chair, and in the name of the Society welcomed Mr. Nicholson as a fellow-townsman, and one who had been instrumental in doing much good in many parts of the world.

Rev. W. J. Wilson, Rev. S. Simms (Belfast), and Mr. J. Goliher (Londonderry) joined in the welcome.

Mr. Nicholson gave a characteristic address, enlivened at the outset by humorous incidents relating to his early life in Bangor. He said it did his heart good to be once more among his own people. He based his address on the subject of "Broken Vessels," and defined sin as any deviation from an absolutely straight path.

From: 'The Life of Faith' – 10th October 1928

THE REV. W. P. NICHOLSON BACK IN THIS COUNTRY (SCOTLAND)

Opening of His Glasgow Campaign after a busy week in the North of Ireland.

The Rev. W. P. Nicholson is again back in this country, and on Sunday night he began an evangelistic campaign in Scotland which will occupy his time and labours until the end of May.

Before proceeding to Glasgow, Mr. Nicholson spent a week in the North of Ireland, the scene of missions about two years ago through which many were led into the Kingdom of God, going there immediately on his arrival from America. Describing the services in Belfast, held under the auspices of the Faith Mission, a correspondent says that on the Saturday a meeting was held to welcome the evangelist back to Ireland.

In the afternoon, he writes, the new large Grosvenor Hall, holding about 2,500 was crowded out before the hour of meetings, and in the evening again the Y.M.C.A. Hall was also packed out long before the advertised time. Hundreds of converts of Mr. Nicholson's previous campaigns attended and gave him a great reception. To those of us who had been with him through these great days, when Belfast and the North of Ireland were moved in a marvellous way by the hand of the Lord upon his honoured servant, we felt as if he was just taking up again where he had left off, and that scenes, such as we had seen on these former occasions would be again repeated.

It was a joy to feel that he is so physically fit again and wonderfully restored in health. His messages, too, had the same deep, gripping, convicting hold upon the people. One was more convinced than ever that his God-honoured success, as well as the hatred he has from the devil and agents, is his loyalty to the Lord Jesus, His Word and the Holy Spirit. He spoke for over an hour in each of the meetings, and held the great audiences to the very end.

(J. B. McLean)

Grosvenor Hall, Belfast c.1927
Courtesy of Belfast Central Mission

Another Belfast correspondent, describing the great meeting held in the Ravenhill Presbyterian Church on Thursday night, under the auspices of the Irish Alliance of Christian Workers' Unions, says the scene there was one of tremendous enthusiasm.

When Mr. Nicholson arrived, it was to find the church packed from door to door, or from gate to gate, with a crowd of over 2,000 people sitting and standing as closely as they possibly could. Long before the doors were opened a crowd had gathered outside, and eventually hundreds had to be turned away.

Representatives were present at the meeting from many of the Unions scattered throughout Ulster. Mr. S. G. Montgomery of Bangor, and President of the I.A.C.W.U. was Chairman. After the twenty-third Psalm had been sung with great vigour and power, and prayer had been offered by the Rev. James Hunter, Messrs. Stevenson (Portadown) and J. Brady (Portglenone) joined with Mr. Montgomery in expressing their delight at seeing their good friend, the Rev. Mr. Nicholson, back in Ireland again. They had not forgotten, they said, the revival and blessing which had come to their country through Mr. Nicholson's efforts a few years ago, and the influence of which was still being felt not only in their own land, but also in other lands. And they hoped, they continued, that the time would not be far distant when Mr. Nicholson would be able to return and take up work amongst them once again. In response to this statement the hundreds crowded into the building rose with one accord to their feet as an indication of their desire also to see this come to pass.

Following this, a powerful and soul stirring address was given by Mr. Nicholson. The message was just such as the world needs today. It was delivered in the power of the Holy Spirit and with extraordinary courage, earnestness and eloquence. There were few hearts unmoved by it. The unique thing about Christianity, it was said, is the cleansing and renewing power which it brings to men and women. This power is able to transform and change the lives of all, but also too often, is it true that those who carry the name of Christ give little evidence of having the power in their lives. There is a strange contradiction between how they live and what the Bible says. And instead of being transformed they are conformed to the world in their habits and lives. They are as much the slaves of worry and bad temper as those around them; they are living for themselves and are powerless and useless in service for God. And as the perplexed and puzzled old world looks on it asks, "Where is your much-talked-of power?"

This state of affairs, the evangelist continued, may be due to one of four reasons. First, it may be due to diversion or to lack of concentration. There is too much activity and running about from meeting to meeting today, and not enough attention given to the development of the inner spiritual life. Again, a multitude of delusions were side-tracking many sincere and good Christian people. Foolish and extravagant notions concerning the Holy Spirit and His work were spoiling and marring the lives of many. And yet, again, others were troubled with a spirit of doubt and fear. They were filled with doubts concerning the reliability of the Bible, doubts concerning the great doctrines of faith, doubts concerning the gracious and wise providence of God. Such people could never be powerful for God. Finally, double dealings with God, Mr. Nicholson said, were a cause of much failure. To be at our best for God we must be honest with Him and true to Him.

For over an hour Mr. Nicholson continued his masterly address, illuminated by many an apt and well-chosen illustration, and still the vast audience listened with unfailing and unwearied attention. Then, as in the closing minutes of his address, minutes so full of the Lord's presence and blessing, the speaker told of the way back to power through repentance and surrender, it was felt that there was a stirring once again of hearts that had grown cold or discouraged in the Master's service, and a coming back and fresh partaking of the invigorating power of the Gospel of Christ.

Mr. Nicholson's friends in Ireland rejoice that the hand of the Lord still rests so mightily upon him; and their constant and fervent prayer is that Scotland may be as much moved for God through His servant as Ireland was a few years ago.

J.A.R.

The Glasgow gatherings began with a Conference on Saturday afternoon, which was not only largely attended and enthusiastic, but was also marked by a deep and earnest purpose, and the note of expectancy found frequent expression. In the minds of all present there was a feeling that an outpouring of blessing is on the way.

Govan Town Hall was crowded on Sunday night, over 2,000 being present. It was a most encouraging start for the campaign, and Mr. Nicholson's stirring address made a deep impression.

Rev. W.P. Nicholson, 1930

1930

NEWSLETTER –3rd January 1930

MAKING "GRANNIES" SING
Rev. W. P. Nicholson's Effort
to Brighten Religion

The Wellington Hall, Y.M.C.A., Belfast, has rarely accommodated such a vast audience as assembled last evening to say farewell to the Rev. W. P. Nicholson. He is going to Los Angeles for a rest cure.

The meeting was a typical "Nicholson" one, and was characterised by the usual bright features which one associates with the well-known evangelist.

For instance he spent over twenty minutes teaching the audience a four-line Gospel song – "I know where I'm going to; do you?" He made men and women sing it separately, and together. He made the women whistle the tune while the menfolk hummed it. His final demand was that all the "grannies" present should sing the verse.

Mr. Nicholson, a bit stouter looking than he was a year or two ago, now wears large horn-rimmed glasses. His hair is nicely parted and well brushed and is not so unruly as in the days of yore.

Otherwise he is the same defiant missioner, and smashes idols right, left and centre. The magnetic personality which moves great crowds in strange ways is not a whit the less.

"Painless Sanctification"

"When I went abroad last time," he remarked with a laugh, "they said I had been kicked out of the country. But this magnificent farewell will spike their guns. Speaking of evangelisation, he said that painless dentistry was a well-known affair, "but," he added "there is no such thing as painless sanctification."

Speaking of the value of union, Mr. Nicholson convulsed the audience with the suggestion that wives should have an eight-hour day, a five-day week, a basic wage, and a bonus for each child.

He concluded with an expression of thanks on behalf of himself and his wife for the kind wishes of his followers.

There were several speakers. Rev. James Hunter, speaking of the value of the work done by Mr. Nicholson, said that if preachers were paid by results, a good many of them would be in the poorhouse.

Rev. Dr. S. Hanna said that the Presbyterian Church in Ireland passed through a very severe crisis in the past three years. That there was no cleavage, he stated, was due to the work done by Mr. Nicholson in the past.

Mr. S. G. Montgomery, whom Mr. Nicholson playfully described as the "Bishop of Bangor," presided.

Belfast Telegraph - 3rd January 1930

"PACIFISM KILLED THE CHURCH"
Rev. W. P. Nicholson's View

Wonderful scenes were witnessed in the Y.M.C.A. Hall, Wellington Place, Belfast, on Thursday evening. The occasion was the departure or rather the return of the Rev. W. P. Nicholson to America. Overstrained by successive evangelistic campaigns in different parts of the world he has been ordered a rest. Hundreds from city, town and country, therefore came to bid him and Mrs. Nicholson farewell, and the doors had to be closed long before the commencement of the meeting.

"Happy Day" and other hymns were used to while away the time; and between them enthusiasm rose to a great height when the Rev. Mr. Nicholson arrived, also the Rev. James Hunter, the Rev. Samuel Hanna, M.B., the Rev. Samuel Simms, Mr. Wm. Dunn, Mr. W. H. Snoddy, and others prominently identified with the Christian Workers' Union and the Bible Standards League. The really impressive moment came when led by the Chairman, Mr. S. G. Montgomery, of Bangor, the whole audience as one great choir rose and sang the 23rd Psalm to the tune Orlington. Apart from the thought of any cause associated with it the effect was magnificent.

The Rev. John Ross having offered prayer, Mr. Montgomery said he had been asked by a man in Bangor how Mr. Nicholson could draw so many people to hear him, and he replied:"First of all Mr. Nicholson is under the sway of Almighty God; and, secondly, he speaks the truth so plainly that everybody can understand it. (Applause). He also loves the souls of the people and aims at directly bringing them to Christ." Their hearts were full of praise and gratitude that God had brought Mr. Nicholson to Ulster in 1920.

Mr. William Millar, formerly Superintendent of Faith Mission work in Ballymena, and now travelling Superintendent and Organiser in connection with Christian Workers' Union, said the people brought to Christ by Mr. Nicholson in that Province and elsewhere were epistles seen and read of all men.

Mr. J. C. Graham, Chairman of the Bible Standards League, referred to the struggle through which they had been passing to maintain the faith that had come down to them. In that struggle he believed Mr. Nicholson had been God's greatest gift.

The Rev. James Hunter, who was welcomed by a perfect storm of applause, spoke of the marvellous results of Mr. Nicholson's campaigns in Ulster.

The Recent Church Crisis

Another speaker to meet with a very warm reception was the Rev. Samuel Hanna, who said they prayed that God might restore Mr. Nicholson and fit him to give Satan a very rough time in the days to come.

In a reference to the struggle through which they had been passing since 1928, he said their Church had been passing through a very serious crisis. He said that without any exaggeration, for he knew that the Presbyterian Church in Ireland had stood as near to a cleavage as she ever would stand until the event took place. Mr. Nicholson's work had averted the event. Mr. Nicholson, like himself, had been barred out of the Assemby Hall, and surely it was only retribution when the very men thought to have been vanquished defeated a subtle scheme. When the history of the period was written it would be found that Mr. Nicholson had done more than anyone in Ulster to keep the Presbyterian Church true to her trust.

In an arresting address Mr. Nicholson said that send-off would be long remembered by his wife and himself. A man had asked him why he could remain a member of the Presbyterian Church in its present state. He replied that he was in the right, and others were in the wrong. These were like cuckoos who had got in to rob the nest. (Laughter). The Lord Bishop of Down, in questioning seventeen candidates for the ministry, found that sixteen of them had been converted at the various missions round the country, and said might the Lord bless the man and the movement. He asked them not to be pacifists. It was accursed pacifism that killed the Church.

1931

Newsletter - 6th January 1931

THE LATE MRS. NICHOLSON (Mother)
Death Follows Eighteen Hours After

The funeral of Mrs. Nicholson, mother of the well-known Ulster evangelist, Rev. W. P. Nicholson, took place from her late residence, "Ellenville," Princetown Road, Bangor, yesterday, to the Old Abbey Graveyard, Bangor.

A service was conducted in the house by Rev. John Ross, Ravenhill Road, Belfast, and Rev. David Dowling, M.A., minister of Trinity Presbyterian Church, Bangor, an the service at the graveside was conducted by Mr. Dowling, Mr. Ross, and Mr. McLean of the Faith Mission, Bangor. Dr. J. C. Nicholson, Hamilton Road, Bangor (son) was the chief mourner at the funeral, which was private. Mrs. Nicholson, who was in her 90th year, had been confined to bed only a few days. Her father was Mr. Ferris Campbell Cottown, Bangor, and she married Capt. J. Nicholson, Merchant Service, over 60 years ago. Her husband died in April 1918. Mrs. Nicholson is survived by Mr. J. Nicholson, chief engineer, s.s. Gatun, Dr. J. C. Nicholson, Bangor; Rev. W. P. Nicholson, Los Angeles (sons), Mrs. Robertson, Manchuria; Mrs. Hanna, Annand, India; and Miss Netta Nicholson (daughters). Another son of Mrs. Nicholson, Mr. Lewis Nicholson, Ormeau Road, Belfast died eighteen hours before his mother.

1936

Belfast Telegraph 21st September 1936

RETURN OF REV. W. P. NICHOLSON
Welcome at Ahoghill
Start of New Campaign

A hearty welcome back to Ulster was given the Rev. W. P. Nicholson and Mrs. Nicholson at Ahoghill on Saturday. It was organised by a number of local friends, in conjunction with the Alliance of Christian Workers' Unions in Ireland and the large assembly, numbering over 1,000 was representative of all the Protestant Churches.

Mr. R. McDermott, President of the Alliance, occupied the Chair, and welcomed Mr. and Mrs. Nicholson on behalf of the Alliance. He emphasised the need of prayer for the success of the new campaign.

Mr. J. B. McLean, Director of the Faith Mission in Ireland, said he had a few red-letter days in his life and some of them in connection with the Rev. W. P. Nicholson's work. It was one of them when he went down on the tender and as him as bright and cheery as of old.

Mr. S. G. Montgomery of Bangor (Mr. Nicholson's native town), said they were expecting to see him there in the not distant future.

Rev. J. Ross, B.A., welcomed them on behalf of Ravenhill Presbyterian Church, and said that the country was in great need of reviving.

Rev. T. Rogers, B.A., of Magheragall Presbyterian Church, thanked God for His servant, and the work that was done years ago.

Mr. Robert Clyde, J.P., one of Ulster's leading businessmen, associated himself with the welcome and urged the necessity for much prayer. The work, he said, might be criticised by others who did not understand, but Christians should go on and not mind these things nor retaliate, and thus perhaps hurt the cause of God.

Rev. A. Fullerton, Lisburn, recalled his association with Mr. Nicholson in his Omagh campaign.

Mr. James Soye joined in the reception on behalf of Lurgan.

Rev. H. H. Murphy, Belfast, said he was the first convert in the Newtownards Mission over a decade ago.

Pastors Freeman and Forbes also spoke words of encouragement, and thanked God for the blessing of the past.

Rev. S.B. Hanna, B.A., M.B., said that before he knew Mr. Nicholson's work he tried to place him and he thought of John the Baptist, but when he got to know it better he just found out that he was W. P. Nicholson. His presence there, he thought, was a miracle after what he had come through in Australia where the doctor had practically given up hope of his recovering. He believed that God had raised him up again because his work was not finished.

Rev. S. Simms from Bethany, Belfast, Mr. F. Mulligan, representing the Belfast City Mission; Mr. G. Gibson, Crossgar, and Mr. W. Millar, organising superintendent of the Alliance, also joined in the welcome.

Mrs. Nicholson said they were glad to be back in Ulster and were grateful to all their friends for their great welcome.

When Mr. Nicholson stood up to say a few concluding words it was some time before he could get speaking owing to the sustained applause. He said that tears had come into his eyes as he came in view of his native land. He was deeply touched by their hearty welcome.

The campaign opened on Sunday at 3 p.m. when again fully 1,000 people gathered.

Mr. Nicholson said that the results of a revival would be conviction of sin in God's people and the putting of wrongs right. Love for one another, love for Christ, and deliverance from worldliness would be other results. Christ satisfied the soul.

Almost 1,500 people crowded the building at the evening meeting and many could not get in.

For nearly an hour the preacher held his audience with an impassioned utterance from Matthew xi., 28 – "Come Ye."

1938

25th January 1938

REV. W. P. NICHOLSON
IN RAVENHILL ROAD CHURCH
Big Crowds Eager to Hear

The Rev. W. P. Nicholson mission in Ravenhill Presbyterian Church, Belfast, is now in full swing, and considering the remarkable personality of the preacher and the power of the message he delivers, the meetings are certain to make a wide appeal.

Mr. Nicholson has travelled over a considerable part of the globe proclaiming the glad news of the Kingdom. He has done this in his own way and after his own method.

No matter how many object to either the one or the other, or to both, of these characteristics, one thing has to be admitted, namely, that he has succeeded where not a few have failed in persuading even the most careless and indifferent to make the great decision.

He has come again to Northern Ireland, the place which above all others he loves best, and great has been the welcome already accorded him. During his stay in the Ravenhill Road Church he is sure to feel quite at home for he is in the midst of old friends.

What is expected to occur while his present mission lasts in that part of the big commercial City of Belfast maybe inferred from the remark of an enthusiastic supporter of such work – "Under the great guns of Nicholson the Devil and his kingdom is certain to experience a terrible rocking!"

Prior to preaching in the Ravenhill Church on Monday evening to packed pews on ground floor and galleries, Mr. Nicholson read the 18th Chapter of Luke's Gospel, which presented well defined portraits of the proud Pharisee and the penitent publican.

His address which followed was a powerful deliverance. He took on the basis of the Scripture mentioned two classes of the unsaved. The first of these was made up of the people whom God could not afford to save. That should soak in and make them think. People were present who were going to hell with all the judgement of God upon them. God could not afford to save them. But there were those whom God could not refrain from saving. While he described those two classes they could know to which they undoubtedly belonged.

The question might be put – Is it possible for God not to be able to afford to save anyone when it was said, "Whosoever?" Were they not among the "Whosoevers?" But God's whosoever was not so wide as they asserted; God's whosoever was limited by the condition – "believeth."

Who then, went on the evangelist, were the people God could not afford to save? First of all the proud. There were more people in hell through pride than through drink or immorality. Pride reached forth its hand and cast down to hell the highest creature Gold had made – the guardian of the Throne of God – Lucifer, son of the morning! God could not afford to save the proud man or woman. Of what were they proud? They were proud of race, proud of place, proud of face, but five minutes after they found themselves in hell there would be very little difference between them and those whom they now despised, but were more openly on the same road to destruction than themselves.

Again, God could not afford to save the self-righteous. They saw that illustrated in the Old Pharisee. Did God save such people; He would risk His holiness, He would risk His justice, He would risk His grace, He would risk His mercy. God could not afford to save that kind of man or woman.

The Way of Salvation

There were people who thought they were saved by loving the Lord and by following the Lord, but they were not saved in that way at all; they were saved by coming as guilty sinners to the feet of God, forsaking their sin, ceasing to have dependence upon their good works, and accepting Christ as their Saviour. When they were saved in that way they could not help loving the Lord and following Him.

The next class God could not afford to save was made up of those of double minds – people who compromised. These people believed they could belong to one organisation or another, one set in society or another, and still belong to God. They clung to the world while affecting to belong to God, and all the time they were on the path to hell.

There was a further class whom God could not afford to save, and that was made up of those who could not break with sin. If they were not going in for a salvation that made them stop sinning, that put hatred of sin and the love and holiness into their hearts, then they could not have God's salvation. There was, lastly, the class that put off the time of decision. The day of salvation was not in the future, but in the eternal present. Mr. Nicholson then proceeded to describe those whom God could not refrain from saving. They were the penitent, the obedient, the believing – those came under the Blood of the Covenant, for the Spirit always answered to the Blood –the confessors of Christ, and the people who did not procrastinate, but made instant decision.

The application came when the preacher asked everyone unsaved in the audience to identify himself or herself with either one or other of the classes portrayed. His closing appeal was answered by a considerable number going into the inquiry room to be dealt with there by Christian workers.

Bright Words – April 1938

AGNES STREET PRESBYTERIAN CHURCH

The Rev. W. P. Nicholson has had a month's intense evangelism in Belfast in Agnes Street Presbyterian Church. From the first meeting onwards, the church has been densely packed (and only those who have been in a Nicholson pack, can realize what this means), every inch of space being occupied, and still large numbers have been unable to gain admission. The evangelist has been at his best, and God has worked mightily through him. He has been kept physically fit too, and miracles have been wrought in many souls passing from death unto life, and there has been revival blessing in the lives of many of God's children.

J. B. McLean

BANGOR CONVENTION – APRIL 14th – 19th

By the time these notes are read, the Bangor Convention will be near at hand. We earnestly ask an interest in your prayers, both in private and in public, for "Except the Lord build the house, they labour in vain that build it." The ultimate object before us is, that God's people may be revived, so that through them "rivers of living water" may flow unhindered.

The speakers now include the Rev. Alexander Frazer and W. P. Nicholson, Messrs. Jock Troup and J. M. Ghaniah (pronounced "Nan-i-ah"). Members of our Council, and others, will take part as opportunities arise. Mr. Nicholson expects to be in the midst of a great Campaign at that time in Lurgan; he has, however, very kindly promised to give us two meetings on Easter Monday at 2.30 and 7.30 p.m. the other speakers, we hope, will be with us for the full period.

J. B. McLean

Belfast Telegraph 7th October 1938

BELFAST TRIBUTE TO REV. & MRS. W. P. NICHOLSON

A large and enthusiastic gathering met in Ravenhill Presbyterian Church on Thursday evening to bid God speed to Rev. W. P. And Mrs Nicholson and to present them with tokens of affection and esteem. The Chair was taken by Mr. R. Simpson.

After a hymn and prayer led by Rev. J. Ross, the chairman said they were gathered to do honour and say farewell to their good friends Rev. W. P. and Mrs. Nicholson. He referred to the great work Mr. Nicholson through God had accomplished in their Province and also in all parts of the world, and that he would best be remembered in the multitude of changed lives. Other speakers were Mr. J. King, C.W.U., Mr. J. B. McLean, Faith Mission, and Rev. J. Ross and Dr. Hanna.

Mrs. King and Mr. Geo. Gibson presented Mr. and Mrs. Nicholson with tokens of esteem. Mr. and Mrs. Nicholson suitably replied and said they were sorry to part with so many loyal friends and hoped to be soon back in their midst.

Mr. Nicholson afterwards gave an address on "The Christian life in the will of God," based on Romans xii., 1 and 2. There were three things about the will of God for their life:- It was good; it was acceptable, it was perfect.

The meeting concluded with the hymn, "Peace, Perfect Peace," and the Benediction. Afterwards the congregation sang "God Be With You Till We Meet Again," and so a happy and profitable meeting was brought to a close.

1940

Rev. W.P. Nicholson, 1940

1946

From: NICHOLSON
1876 – Centenary – 1976 by Rev. Ian R. K. Paisley

Nicholson the Unpredictable Man

On the Sunday after I was ordained on this road, 1st August, 1946, to my amazement, in my first morning service, W. P. Nicholson was in the back seat of the church. I was a mere stripling of twenty. I had sat in W. P. Nicholson's great meetings in the early thirties. I had sat at his feet, as a boy, in what was known as the "Ahoghill Cathedral" when he preached to vast crowds of people.

I need not tell you I was nervous. After I had finished, the great preacher walked up to the front of the church. He said, "I have one prayer I want to offer for this young man. I will pray that God will give him a tongue like an old cow." And he said, "Go in, young man, to a butcher's shop and ask to see a cow's tongue. You will find it is sharper than any file. God give you such a tongue. Make this church a converting shop and make this preacher a disturber of Hell and the Devil." I well remember him standing there and uttering those words.

I believe God answered his prayer, for my tongue has caused great trouble to Popes and Popery, Ecumenists and Ecumenicalism, Modernists and Modernism and by the grace of God I have disturbed the Devil on this road and will continue to be a DD, a Devil Disturber, in this area. By the help of Heaven!

W. P. Nicholson was unpredictable in his pulpit and ministration.

A woman came to him once and said, "Sir, my husband beats me." He said, "I can easily remedy that. Get him to the service." She said, "I will do my best." He said, "The night you are in the service and he is with you, give me a nod and I will know he is there." And sure enough one night the woman was there and a man was sitting beside her. She gave the preacher a nod. He nodded back. When it came to the offering the preacher said, "I have somewhat to say. There is a man in this meeting who beats his wife. What a dirty coward and rascal he is." Then he gave this man, without mentioning him, a terrible dressing down. "Now I am prepared to be generous" he said, "as the plate is passed I will watch what that man gives and if he does not put on a ten shilling note, I will name him after the offering is lifted." That night the plates were cluttered with ten shilling notes!

Once in Rosemary Street Church, as he was preaching, a drunk man disturbed the meeting. Nicholson told him to shut up or he would throw him out. The man continued to disturb the meeting. So Nicholson had the congregation singing, and he left the pulpit and went down and caught the man by the scruff of the neck, opened the church door and threw him into the middle of Rosemary Street. He slammed the door, and as he was walking up the aisle a woman said to him, "Mr. Nicholson, the Saviour would not have done that." "No," says Nicholson, "The Saviour would have cast the devil out of the man. I cannot do that Madam, I did the second best thing, I cast the devil out and the man out as well."

Rev. John Pollock of St. Enoch's comments: "Some of the things he says sound bad when read in cold type, but they 'taste good' when accompanied by his genial smile, which sometimes breaks into a loud and most infectious guffaw. He is a genuine humorist and knows well how to substantiate the saying 'he who laughs is not far from tears.' I have seen his vast audiences convulsed with laughter, and cheering uproariously, and within ten seconds sitting in solemn stillness under the spell of his pathos."

I told you about his great meeting in Lurgan. The Town Clerk of Lurgan was a Christian. He was entirely bald! He had not a hair on his head. He had a bad habit of coming to church late. W. P. Nicholson did not like latecomers. (And I see Mr. Nesbitt smiling, as he was one of his stewards – he very well knows!) So one night the Presbyterian Church was packed, and here comes in the bald Town Clerk of Lurgan. He walks into the aisle and he looks all round for a seat. Nicholson stops the meeting and says, "Hi man, it was not combing your hair that kept you late."

I remember once in the "Ahoghill Cathedral" when the place was packed, that a young lady came in and she was wearing an outrageous yellow frock. There were two elderly women in the front seat and they were spread along the seat. This young lassie could not get a seat. I saw W. P. Nicholson smile and he looked down at the two women in the front seat and he said, "If you two clocking hens would pull in your wings that canary could get in beside you."

I told you about the great campaign in Newtownards. The interest in that campaign was sparked off with an incident that took place at its beginning. The main employer of labour, the owner of the factory in Newtownards was a Christian and so was his daughter. They were very wealthy. One night at the beginning of the campaign when the place was packed, this man's daughter came in and she had on a white fur coat, a most unusual coat. W. P. Nicholson looked at her and he stopped the meeting, and he cried out, "Hi boys, look what has come in. I thought polar bears were at the North Pole, but there is one in Newtownards and it has come to my mission." Do you know that the hard workmen in that factory, in a day when labour had its differences with the directors of the firm, when they heard that a preacher had called down the employer's daughter in such language, they came in their hundreds and, praise God, hundreds of them were born gain.

There was method in what the evangelist was doing! I remember my father showing me a letter in which he had invited W.P. Nicholson to come and take a meeting for him. The great preacher wrote back and said, "Dear Brother Paisley, I am like a flea on an Irishman's back, I am always jumping. Sorry I cannot jump your way. Yours respectfully busy, W. P. Nicholson," Typical of the man!

From: 'A Local Perspective' – W. P. Nicholson by Ken McFall September 1946

CARRICKFERGUS MISSION

On hearing of Rev. W. P. Nicholson's return from the U.S.A., Jonathan Simms, the young secretary of Y.P.C.L., wrote to him on behalf of the committee, with a view to organising a Gospel campaign in the town. A positive response swung the organising committee into action and their next task was to find a suitable church in which to hold the mission. First Presbyterian Church, which had been the choice for his last successful campaign in 1923, seemed an ideal venue, and if approved by the Church, the mission could be under way by Autumn.

A deputation from the Young People's Christian League arrived at the church session meeting to request the use of the church and were met by the minister in charge, Rev. Robert Caldwell. He requested the deputation to retire for a short while to allow time to discuss the matter.

This short 'while' turned into an anxious wait. Could a response to their request really take as long as this? The deputation had a mission to organise and time was of paramount importance. Just then a footstep indicated the return of Rev. Caldwell.

"A decision," he said, "had been reached," It appeared their wait was not in vain, although his response did take a little while to sink in at first. The Rev. Caldwell who presided over the meeting, spoke on behalf of the church.

"We have agreed in the affirmative for the use of our Church."

This was the message which propelled the September Mission into top gear. Once again First Presbyterian Church would host a campaign, heralding from its pulpit the message of salvation through Christ and it would also see the return of W. P. Nicholson, by now a world-renowned evangelist.

Salvation Army Band

As for the 1923 Mission there were plenty of tasks to be undertaken in preparation for such an event. A prayer meeting topped the list, being organised weeks in advance of Rev. Nicholson's arrival in the town.

On the Saturday night prior to the opening Sunday evening, a welcoming meeting was organised when a Salvation Army Band from Belfast was present. No effort would be spared in advertising the mission, so the band proceeded to lead a parade around the town, giving advanced notice, that the mission would commence the next evening.

Ill Health

When Rev. W. P. Nicholson came to Carrickfergus in September 1946 he was five months over his seventieth birthday. While still going strong, health problems were beginning to take their toll on his life and became the deciding factor for the duration of the mission, so the organizing committee decided on only two weeks. Accommodation for Rev. and Mrs. Nicholson was arranged. He would travel by his own car, staying at Cable Road in Whitehead. Occasionally Mrs. Nicholson would relieve, W. P. by driving him, but on all other occasions he drove himself. He once remarked, "Driving helps me to relax and takes my thoughts away from continually dwelling upon the mission."

Caring Touch

On the opening night he arrived smartly dressed in his black jacket and white shirt, complete with his round rimmed glasses. His face shone as he took up his position in the pulpit. He was 'well built', a jolly type, but small in stature with a portly figure. There was an unmistakable caring nature and touch about him – a down-to-earth man. No one could ever suggest differently, he could never be accused of being an impostor, his look spoke of genuineness.

On the opening Sunday night, 1st September 1946, those gathered in the Church occupied every available pew. A prayer meeting, in session from 7.15p.m., pleaded for the divine presence of God and help for the preacher in the meeting to follow at 8.30 p.m. The meeting, in the usual Nicholson style, commenced promptly at the hour of 8.30p.m. Rev. W. P. Nicholson took full charge of the service, launching straight into a number of lively hymns, before committing the mission to God in prayer. He believed in good hymn singing, for he once said it would relieve the people from their stress, worries and cares of life. Only then, after this rendering of praise before God, would Nicholson finally begin to preach the Gospel of saving grace to an aroused and waiting congregation. Night after night the format didn't seem to change much. Praise and thanksgiving to a Holy God were the most consistent hallmarks of his meetings. He was unrelenting in his messages and the proclamation of the Good News of his Saviour, and the power of Christ's blood in cleansing away sin appeared to be endless.

The prayer meetings before the mission were very soon augmented by an after-church prayer time which continued nightly, starting at 9.30 p.m. and sometimes lasting to midnight and beyond. The organisers were joined by many of God's people in these times of intercessions when Rev. Nicholson could be heard weeping for the town and the souls of its people.

At the conclusion of this mission, conversions ran into a few hundred, not the large results of the 1923 Mission, but equally successful in many ways, for again, hundreds of souls found their way to Calvary.

'The Christian' – 10th October 1946

Rev. W. P. Nicholson
Mission at Carrickfergus
(Report)

Twenty-three years ago Rev. W. P. Nicholson visited Carrickfergus, and in our recollection the experiences of that time live as though they occurred yesterday. The power of God was with the preaching and the place was shaken. Some of the older folk said they had known nothing like it since the days of Moody.

Recently, he returned to the town and conducted another stirring campaign in the First Presbyterian Church, founded in 1621, and the oldest Presbyterian Church in Ireland. At the opening service Mr. Nicholson was welcomed by Mr. Charles Hilditch who, at the age of ten, accepted Christ during the earlier mission referred to. The evangelist said that during forty-seven years' campaigning he never knew a mission "so soaked in prayer." Every morning at six o'clock a goodly company met in the Y.M.C.A. for prayer, and twice there were protracted evening prayer meetings.

Mr. Nicholson is unusual and a man to whom no one seems to be indifferent and always there goes with him a band of men whose hearts the Lord has touched. His critics have not always had the logic of those of whom it was said that beholding the man which was healed standing with them," they could say nothing against it."

In our friend's preaching there is power and pathos; his message wounds because of its faithfulness, and heals because of its tenderness.

His hearers are not an emotional people; here, if anywhere in the North of Ireland, we have the Ulster Scot. It is unwise to count the number of those who profess acceptance of the Saviour. Suffice it to say that sometimes during the mission the nets were breaking; there were more "in the valley of decision" than there were workers to guide them; there was a beckoning to others "that they should come and help them." On one night the ages of the men inquirers ranged from seventeen to thirty-two, and the records as a whole show that between the ages of ten and fifty-five all types of personality passed through. Mrs. Nicholson and Mrs. Leslie were in charge of the women's inquiry room.

1947

**From: 'Glad Tidings' (I.A.C.W.U. Magazine) Issue 9
ENNISKILLEN
Personal Testimony of Mr. Denzil McIlfatrick**

*'I know whom I have believed, and am persuaded that He is able to
keep that which I have committed unto Him against that day." (2 Tim.1:12)*

This verse of scripture became a reality to me when I was Saved on Friday, 21st February, 1947.

My eldest brother Bill was Saved in 1939, and his life made a tremendous impact on me. He was among the first students at the newly formed Belfast Bible School during the War years. He was accepted to O.M.S. (International) for missionary service in India. A month before my brother sailed for India in March 1947, he helped the Rev. W. P. Nicholson in a mission in the Presbyterian Church, Enniskillen.

My brother invited me to this mission and I went one night during the second week. I felt so uncomfortable spiritually in the meeting that I was reluctant to go back.

Towards the end of the final week my brother was getting very anxious that I should hear Mr. Nicholson once more. On the last Friday night of the mission I had on my uniform as a Scout Leader and was about to leave home. My brother challenged me about going to the mission, saying, "You may never have another opportunity like this!" Somehow, the way he said, "You may never have another opportunity like this!" seemed to have a real note of conviction about it, so I changed my uniform and went to the mission.

When I went into the church there were very few empty seats. Just then Mr. Nicholson got up and asked if several young people would come to the front. A steward caught my arm and brought me up to a seat in the pulpit beside Mr. Nicholson. When I sat down I felt most embarrassed, especially when I saw so many people I knew.

After the hymn singing and the preliminaries, Mr. Nicholson read the scripture. He then announced his text: Genesis 6:3 "And the Lord said, My Spirit shall not always strive with man..." He said: "I am going to speak on the Unpardonable Sin; the sin that has no forgiveness in this world, or in the world that is to come."

As Mr. Nicholson preached, the Spirit of God began to work in my heart. I felt a real deep conviction, such as I had never experienced in my life before. It seemed to me that it was a now, or never, as far as me accepting the Lord Jesus Christ as my Saviour was concerned.

Mr. Nicholson kept reminding us of the danger of grieving the Holy Spirit, saying there could come a time when He would cease to strive. If that happened, then it would not be possible to get Saved. He told of Esau, who sold his birthright, not being able to find a place for repentance, even though he sought it diligently with tears.

As Mr. Nicholson came to the end of his message I was convinced that if I did not come to the Lord Jesus Christ then, I would never again feel the same about the need of Salvation. During the singing of the last hymn, 'Just as I am' Mr. Nicholson asked us to keep our seats. He then asked those who wanted to take Jesus as their Saviour to stand during the singing of the hymn. A great conflict raged in my soul, and I reached the point where I was not even conscious of the large congregation sitting below me. I was face to face with the greatest crisis of my life and the decision was mine and mine alone.

I stood to my feet, and a great burden rolled from my soul. As I was immediately behind Mr. Nicholson, he did not see me stand. Someone down in the congregation indicated to him that I had stood up. He turned round and said: "God bless you young man."

That night was the happiest in my whole life. Sleep did not come easy, because of the peace and joy that filled my soul.

As quite a number of those associated with the Irish Evangelistic Band assisted in the mission, I became involved in this work which helped me tremendously in the early years of my spiritual growth.

On the 10th Anniversary of my Conversion I wrote a letter of appreciation to Mr. Nicholson for all that his ministry meant to me. Here is an extract from the letter he sent in reply:

"....God bless you all and keep you from ever getting used to men going to hell, but by all means all the time, saving some. It is so easy these days to become lukewarm.

I am glad you have experienced the 'Second Touch'. There is no substitute for a Spirit Baptised Sanctified experience if we are to live holy lives of victory and satisfaction and successful soul winning service.

....I must close Dear Brother! Keep nothing back from the Lord Jesus. Let Him have All, Always. Jesus never fails, NEVER! Hallelujah! May you ever be a terrible nuisance to the devil and a delight to God. Maranatha! Hallelujah!"

Sloan Street Presbyterian Church, Lisburn (left of picture) where
the Great United Evangelistic Campaign took place in November 1947

Courtesy of Irish Linen Centre and Lisburn Museum

The Lisburn Standard 14th November 1947

W. P. NICHOLSON
Evangelistic Campaign Draws Large Congregations

So great was the attendance at the evening session of the United Evangelistic Campaign conducted by the Rev. W. P. Nicholson, the well known evangelist, in Sloan Street Presbyterian Church on Sunday night that extra seating accommodation had to be provided. Chairs and forms were installed in all the aisles and forms also conveyed upstairs to the gallery so large was the congregation.

The Rev. Mr. Nicholson, who conducted the service as well as deliver the address, led in the chorus singing before the service commenced, his robust voice and commanding personality playing a great part in the success of the singing. He invited various sections of the congregation to sing choruses in turn, also the ladies and men to take turns at singing the refrains.

Mr. Nicholson told his audience that he was delighted to be back in Lisburn. He had conducted a campaign in Lisburn 25 years ago and the revival had been a most memorable one. But he had a regret regarding that campaign – he was not invited back to Lisburn. Indeed of all the towns in the Province he had visited, Lisburn was the one town where he was not invited back. He wondered why? At any rate he was back again in that famous town and was delighted to have the opportunity of addressing the local listeners once again.

Mr. Nicholson who read a portion of Scripture, prefaced his reading by saying that people to-day had varied conceptions of Christ's appearance. Some believed he was a big man, some even hazarded guesses as to his dress, appearance, timbre of his voice etc., but he could say that all the pictures and statues in existence were purely examples of Roman Popery. No one knew what Christ looked like, what his appearance was, or how he spoke. God saw to that. But we had before us the very words He uttered two thousand years ago and that was all we needed to help us to enter into the ways of Christ.

Mr. Nicholson, who preached for about half an hour, chose the words "Come, tarry and go" for his theme, and drew a graphic picture for his audience of how to find God. Some people thought they had found Christ, but they were merely doping themselves with spiritual complacency, and were the victims of their own stupidity. He appealed to his congregation to try to learn the true message of God and He would open up new paths of righteousness if they only had the will to follow.

The Campaign which continued each night during the week not only attracted large and enthusiastic congregations and proved an unqualified success but was a signal tribute to the abilities of inimitable Mr. Nicholson who, making his return to Lisburn after a quarter of a century, has lost none of his great genius for evangelistic preaching.

Welcome Tea

A tea to welcome the Rev. W. P. Nicholson and Mrs. Nicholson to Lisburn was given in the C.W.U. Hall, Market Street, on Saturday afternoon, the presence of the United Committee and numerous friends greatly adding to the success of the function.

Mr. T. Cregan (Chairman of the United Committee) who presided, spoke of how they had looked forward to the visit of the Rev. Mr. Nicholson, and said they were convinced the campaign would be rewarded with great spiritual blessing.

Speeches of welcome were made by Rev. A. Fullerton, Rev. T. G. Keery, Rev. W. Kennedy, M.A., Rev. N. E. Mulligan, M.B.E., Pastor Thompson and Messrs. S. B. McCleery, J. R. Grant and W. Houston (Ahoghill) D. McCready, W. Collins, J. Curry (Portadown) A. Maze, V. McAfee, W. Stafford, F. Campbell and Mr. Mitchell (Belfast).

Mr. and Mrs. Nicholson then spoke and thanked all for the cordial welcome and good wishes.

The Lisburn Standard –28th November 1947

Evangelistic Campaign

This weekend will bring to a close the great United Evangelistic Campaign, conducted by Rev. Wm. P. Nicholson, that has been attracting crowded congregations to Sloan Street Presbyterian Church, Lisburn, for the past three weeks.

The mission never lacked interest from the commencement, great numbers of people attending each evening from Ahoghill, Ballymena, Ballygowan, Saintfield, Ballynahinch, Dromara, Magheragall, Crumlin, Colin, Stoneyford and Belfast.

The Rev. Mr. Nicholson and his wife have been accorded much material and spiritual support during the campaign and will leave Lisburn with the prayers and best wishes of the entire community.

LISBURN AND DISTRICT MONTHLY HOLINESS MEETING (INTERDENOMINATIONAL)

SPEAKER AT THE
DECEMBER MONTHLY MEETING

REV. W. P. NICHOLSON

IN FRIENDS' MEETING HOUSE
RAILWAY STREET, LISBURN
(kindly granted)

ON MONDAY NEXT 1ST DECEMBER, 1947 AT 8 O'CLOCK P.M.

Ulster's own Evangelist, whose ministry God has used to the Salvation and sanctification of multitudes

Come and hear more about this full salvation which not only CLEANSES from the GUILT, but SAVES from the POWER of sin.

Doors Open 7 o'clock   Prayer Meeting 7.15
ALL WELCOME

HOLINESS MEETING
Large Audience Hears Rev. W. P. Nicholson's Message

The December Monthly Holiness Meeting proved to be the climax to the mission which has just concluded in Sloan Street Church under the auspices of the C.W.U. and which was conducted by the well known evangelist, Rev. W.P. Nicholson. A large congregation packed the Friends' Meeting House of which the greater part was men.

Hymns which had been favourites during the Mission were sung, and prayer was offered by Mr. W. Collins. Welcoming the Rev. Mr. Nicholson, Mr. Smartt, on behalf of the Holiness Committee, expressed their indebtedness to the speaker for consenting to stay over for a further night after such a strenuous mission, and said what a privilege it was to have him address the meeting. He also voiced the committee's thanks to the committee of the Friends' Meeting House for the use of their beautiful building in which the monthly meetings had been held for the past year, and which was ideal for the purpose.

Rev. Mr. Nicholson, who said he felt very much at home, as indeed he always did in a holiness meeting, took for his subject "Ten reasons why I believe with all my heart in holiness. And giving chapter and verse for the benefit of Bible students quoted the following: (1) It is God's choice; (2) It is God's call; (3) It is God's will; (4) It is God's command; (5) It is God's gift; (6) Christ died to accomplish it; (7) The Holy Spirit is the witness to it; (8) God is not ashamed of it; (9) Paul prayed that we might have it; and (10) Without it no man could see God. With his own inimitable directness of speech, Mr. Nicholson showed clearly that holiness and healthiness are one and the same thing, and there was not a Christian present who could fail to comprehend the necessity for a holy life.

When the appeal was made a good number expressed their willingness to claim the blessing of sanctification, and the meeting closed with the hymn "Have Thine own way, Lord," and the Benediction.

Friends' Meeting House - Railway Street, Lisburn

1948

**Rev. Wm. P. Nicholson's
Itinerary
1948**

Dear Prayer Partners,

This is an outline of our itinerary for 1948 (D.V.) and a wee reminder to help us in the fight, by your prayers and intercession. We can do without many things, but we can't do without your constant prayers. So please do not let us down. "Pray with unceasing prayer and entreaty on every fitting occasion in the Spirit and be always on the alert to seek opportunities for doing so, with unwearied persistence and entreaty, on behalf of all God's people, and ask on our behalf, that words may be given to us, so that, outspoken and fearless, we may make known the truths of the good news, so that when telling them we may speak out boldly as we ought."

Yours in His service,

Wm. P. and F. E. NICHOLSON
John 3.30

Itinerary, 1948

BALLYMENA	-	January 4 – 25
MAGHERA	-	February 8 – 29
OLDHAM, (Eng.)	-	March 26 – April 11
RASHARKIN	-	April 18 – May 10
BALLYNAHINCH	-	May 23 – June 13
LISNASKEA	-	June 20 – July 11
PORTRUSH C.W.U.		
CONVENTION	-	August
LONDONDERRY	-	September 5 – 26
NEWRY	-	October 3 – October 24
BANGOR	-	October 31 – November 21
CORK	-	November 28 – December 19

LETTERS TO LISBURN

January 1949 - December 1951

During his ministry Rev. and Mrs. Nicholson often stayed at "Elmwood" on the Belsize Road, Lisburn, the home of Mr. and Mrs. Chittick who owned a drapery shop in Bow Street. The following are (unedited) personal letters written by Mr. Nicholson to his friends while he travelled abroad. *(published with permission)*

Rev. Wm. P. Nicholson

Queen's Park Hotel.
Balaiea Drive
Queen's Park.
Glasgow. S.2.
16th January 1949.

Dear Mr Chittick:-

I enclose 14 "E" coupons which expire end of Jany. You said to send them to you & you would get them exchanged for others which can be used while we are over with you during February (D.V.) We will have a lot of running around ere we sail for Liverpool March 4, so will require the most if not all of them. Don't bother sending them over, I can get them when we arrive. I have Basic ones that will keep me going here.

How is Mr Chittick & the wee "bairn"? We hope both are making satisfactory progress & will soon be home. There'll be queer excitement amongst the children to see their new wee sister.

We had a wonderful break last night (Tuesday) some 50 or more come right out to the front for Full salvation. Boys! what a time we had. You might heard us in Lisburn. Every meeting members of families are deciding for Christ, & the end is not yet. Hallelujah! We are both well but very tired & looking forward to a good rest at "Elmwood" ere we sail. (D.V.) We will be with you Tuesday (1st Feby) as soon as ever I can get our Car after arrival. See III John 13 - 14.

Much love from us both to you all & thanking you for your many kindly kindnesses to us.

Yours as ever for ever.
Wm. P. Nicholson jnr 3d.

16th January 1949
Glasgow, 2.

Dear Mr. Chittick

I enclose 14 "E" Coupons which expire end of January. You said to send them to you and you would get them exchanged for others which can be used while we are over with you during February (D.V.) We will have a lot of running around ere we sail for Liverpool March 4, so will require the most if not all of them. Don't bother sending them over, I can get them when we arrive. I have basic ones that will keep me going here.

How is Mrs. Chittick and the wee "Ewe Lamb"? We hope both are making satisfactory progress and will soon be home. There'll be queer excitement amongst the children to see their new wee sister.

We had a wonderful break last night (Tuesday) some 50 or more come right out to the front for Full Salvation. Boys! What a time we had. You might have heard us in Lisburn. Every meeting numbers of sinners are deciding for Christ, and the end is not yet. Hallelujah! We are both well but very tired and looking forward to a good rest at "Elmwood" ere we sail (D.V.) We will be with you Tuesday (1st February) as soon as ever we can get our car after arrival. See III John 13 –14.

Much love from us both to you all and thanking you for your many kindly kindnesses to us.

> *Yours as Ever forever,*
> **Wm. P. Nicholson, Jn. 3.30.**

(Note – the 'Ewe Lamb' spoken of was new baby daughter Esther Elizabeth. Mr. and Mrs. Nicholson accompanied Mr. and Mrs. Chittick on the homeward journey from hospital. The baby's second name 'Elizabeth' was called after Mrs. Nicholson.)

Nicholson Mission

Being convinced that I am a sinner, I **now** accept Jesus Christ as my own personal **Saviour,** and promise in humble dependence on the Holy Spirit to confess Him as my **Lord,** and I desire with my whole heart to live as His obedient servant all my life.

Name... *Mrs Chittick*

Address... *Bow St. Lisburn*

Date... *12th April 1938*

"O Son of God who lovest me,   And all I have, and all I am,
I will be Thine alone,   Shall henceforth be thine own."

"The Son of God Who loved me and gave Himself for me."
Gal. 2: 20.

March 12th 1949
Dakar, West Africa

Dear Mr and Mrs Chittick

It was a queer sore experience saying Goodbye to all you dear friends. The "holy water" wasn't far away nor scarce. The life of the evangelist is one continuous greeting and partings. Praise God! We are bound for the land of the pure and the holy where we'll meet to part no more. We had a lovely crossing to Liverpool, but Boys! What a reception. A real good, old-fashioned snow storm. Thick and heavy and strong. But once we were aboard we were nice and cosy. All the cabins and lounges are steam heated. We have such a nice big roomy cabin. There are only 30 passengers on board. She is 12,000 tons, so we have any amount of room and quiet.

The Captain is a Belfast man and lives in Ballymena when home (Captain Brown). Mrs. Nicholson has been seasick for 4 days but is up and about again. I have been laid low with another attack of bronchitis, but feeling better again now we are having nice warm weather. It feels good the cold and wet of dear old Ulster.

We expect to arrive at Dakar this evening. We don't stay long there. We refuel with oil and sail again on Sunday morning. We are not sure yet whether we will be allowed ashore. This is a Yellow Fever district. From all I hear we won't miss much, as there is not much to see.

Wouldn't it be fine if you were all on board here with us. We wouldn't feel so lonesome. We will never forget all the kindnesses you showered on us while we were your guests. Never. God bless you and all yours for it all.

This is just a wee note to let you know our whereabouts and our love for you all. I will write more fully ere we get to Cape Town (D.V.). We hope you all keep well and cheerie. Love to you all (the real sort).

Mrs. Nicholson joins me in all this.

> *Yours and His*
> **Wm. P. Nicholson Jn.3.30.**
Remember us to all mutual friends.

6th January 1950
Australia, N.S.W

Dear Mr. and Mrs. Chittick

The two boxes of collars arrived and we received them today. They are lovely, fit like a glove. Many, many thanks. They'll last me until Jesus Comes or I get my "Home Call".

Laugh at this – a friend took the Customs card to the office. The parcel was opened. The man said £4.10.0. and duty would be £1.10.0. He then came across your letter and said "Rev." He said, "Oh, for Rev. Nicholson from Ireland". He took the card to another man and came back and said "Seeing it was "Rev." and from Ireland they would put the value at £1 and duty 6/9. "Oh what a change!" You see, most government offices are filled with R.C.s They thought I was a Priest. So I am, but not a R.C. one I am a Roaming Catholic. This is one on the dirty old Pope. "Up Ulster!"

The rug hasn't arrived yet. I hope you have "REV" conspicuous on the parcel. You are far too kind to us. We could never repay you for all your many kindnesses, but we are not ungrateful. Our hearts are full of gratitude.

We are having it very hot here and very humid. It is sore on me and I find breathing hard. We have just finished a Convention at Katoomba 3,750 ft altitude. Blue Mountains. We had a great 10 days. Over 200 out for Full Salvation and scores of sinners converted. Hallelujah! Unto Him be all the Glory.

I managed to stay during the 10 days and preached nearly every day, but I had a hard time. I couldn't get my breath. Mrs. N's wee pills were my salvation. I am glad to be down at sea level again. We are resting all January. We were very homesick Christmas Day. We were in and around "Elmwood" that day and other places too. We felt a wee bit lonesome.

We hope you had a good Christmas in spite of the cold and colds. We hope you are fully recovered from the cold. Poor wee Christopher. We trust he is OK again and minding things.

We have had an election here and chucked overboard the R.C., Communist, labour crew. We have a liberal one now. Things will be better, but they left a queer mess to be cleared up. I hope you'll get rid of the Atlea gang next election. They'd ruin any country with their wildcat schemes and destruction of private enterprize.

Glad you had good Holiness meetings and that Union meetings are going fine. Remember us to Bull Dog and all the other friends. Tell them to pray hard for us.

I wonder have we sent you our 1950 Itinerary. I will send one in another envelope and a snap of us and car. I must close. Much love (the real sort) from us both to you all. God bless you all. We love you and pray for you, as I know you do us. Keep believing and rejoicing.

Yours restfully busy
Wm. P. Nicholson Jn.3.30.

7th April 1950
Australia, N.S.W.

Dear Mr. and Mrs. Chittick

Your good letters received and read and discussed. You do write good letters, so long and full of news and all about "Elmwood". "Birds singing. Not so many bees. Molly on holiday and all of you colds now and then." We just sit as we read and see it all and do you know a wee tug comes to our hearts! Wouldn't it be fine if we could go over there again. "Oh Boys!" I don't think it possible at my time of life (I was 74 the other day).

As soon as we finish here we will sail for California (D.V.) settle down there and soak sunshine and drink good desert air, until the Call comes, or the Trumpet sounds. We will never forget all your love and kindness to us. It was just at a time when we seemed to be tumbled about concerning a home, and some friends forsaking us, you were brought into our lives. It was a glad day for us. I have wee Chris's photo on our looking glass and every time I see it my heart rises in prayer for you all and we say heartily "God bless the Chitticks".

Our summer here is almost over and we're not sorry. The heat is so sore on you owing to humidity. We have been having unprecedented rain and floods. Great loss of life, property and cattle. Places where they haven't had rains for years, are floods. Then there are Strikers everywhere, every day. Communist led. The Government seems scared of them. There's queer unrest and dissatisfaction and hatred on every hand. Big wages and rising prices and mens hearts failing them for fear. Friends! There's only one way out of it all, and that is Up. Hallelujah! It can't be long until we hear the Shout. The Lord is blessing and goodly numbers are Coming to Christ and believers being sanctified, so we're not downhearted. But we long for revival greatly. We leave for Melbourne next week (D.V.) 600 miles South. Our Austin 16 H.9 runs like a sewing machine.

The roads have been washed out. We hope they may be repaired ere we travel. We may be hindered going to Q'land owing to roads, weather most distances. No! We won't be in New Zealand this trip and maybe never again.

You say Mr. Laidlow would be in Ulster in August. We are to meet him tomorrow here. He will be in the city for some days preaching. Glad the C.W.U. meetings are going well and your Holiness meeting. Remember us to our mutual friends. Glad "Bull Dog" is going strong, give him our love and the Smarts. We are both well and glad we are able to work and travel. The Lord our God is good. We can never trust Him too much or ourselves too little.

God bless you all richly. We love you and pray for you every day. Keep believing and singing.

> *Yours restfully busy*
> **Wm. P. Nicholson, Jn. 3.30**

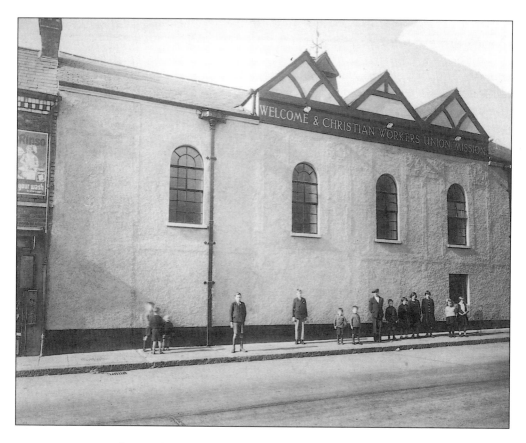

The Welcome & Christian Workers' Union Hall
Market Street, Lisburn

Courtesy of Irish Linen Centre

Seymour Street, Lisburn in the 1950s – keeping left at the end of this street led to the Belsize Road and the home of the Chitticks

Courtesy of Belfast Telegraph c.1954

12th August 1950
Australia N.S.W.

Dear Mr. and Mrs. Chittick

The parcel of refills arrived safe and sound. Not one injured. They could hardly be hurt the wonderful way you packed them. I wondered what on earth the packet contained. As I unrolled roll after roll of cotton wool I began to think some one was playing a joke on me. Then I came to the refills. Boys! You could almost have heard me shout. I was so glad. I did say from my heart. God bless the Chitticks. You are so kind and generous. You have been that to us ever since we knew you. We often say "We wish we had known you sooner" for we had been kicked around from one boarding house to another. We wandered far and wide seeking a place to live. Oh dear! But sometimes we were down in the dumps. Then we were led to you dear people. Happy day! We relive over and over again the happy days we spent at "Elmwood". I wonder will we ever have another such time ere He comes or we pass on? I wonder. Now here I am blethering and never said "Thank you" for going to all the trouble and expense. I wish you would let me refund you the amount of the refills. I know its no use saying a word about that. I am about my last letter in my last refill. Every time I take my pen to write, I'll be sure and say "God bless the Chitticks". Of course we pray for you regularly. Then the newspapers were fine. Even the smell of them did us good.

The most and worst of our winter is past. It has been so cold and wet. Rains unprecedented. Floods and great loss of lives, property, cattle and sheep. Weeks on end and never a dry day. One wonders if God had forgotten about the Rainbow and His promise. Towns and cattle had to be fed by aeroplanes dropping the stuff to them. We escaped the flu. It was an epidemic until 2 weeks ago. I went down with bronchitis and verging on pneumonia. Then sciatica in both limbs. High temperature. My old heart began to weaken. So I am ordered complete rest and had to cancel the mission. Wow! Wow! But ANYHOW! Hallelujah! I had a good nurse day and night, and Dr. and best of all, such a wonderful Saviour. I am up again, but feeling dottery on my feet. These are sunny days and we have a wee drive out in it, so I am fit as a fiddle and as good as 10 dead ones. I had a chest like a <u>Twelfth</u> July drum.

Mrs. N. Keeps well, rules me like a tyrant. God bless her. I love her all the more. Remember us to all mutual friends. We hope you are all well and cheerie. God richly bless you all always.

Mrs. Nicholson joins me in much love (the <u>real</u> sort) to you both. Pray for us as we do for you every day. Keep believing.

> *Yours busily resting.*
> **Wm. P. Nicholson Jn. 3.30**

25th December 1951
California, U.S.A.

Dear Mr. and Mrs. Chittick

Your long and newsy letter received and read and discussed. It was just like dropping into "Elmwood" and having a good chat, but we couldn't have a wee drop of tea. You must have had an anxious time about the wee baby, but glad it is all over. I like that clause so frequently used in the Bible "And it came to pass". It didn't come to stay." Hallelujah!

You must be having a real winter over there. In the Mid Western and Eastern States here they are having the worst winter they can remember. Such zero weather. Snow storms and many deaths. It makes us very glad and thankful we are living here in Sunny Southern California. We have had unusual weather for here. We have had 5 to 6 inches of rain and some nights down to freezing. But during the day around 70 degrees and mostly sunny.

Maybe we wouldn't be glad if you all come out here. It is easier entering the Kingdom of Heaven than getting into U.S.A. I believe the quota is filled and a 5 year waiting list. If you flew over you could only stay 6 months. I remember when you could travel anywhere and it was nobody's business, but not these days.

Your lovely Christmas present arrived. Thank you very much. You are far too kind to us. We spread it on our table today (Christmas). It looked so lovely and we felt as if you were here. We had our Christmas all by ourselves. The children and grandchildren (And I say! I am a GREAT grand dad) held their Christmas in their own homes. So we had a nice quiet time alone, and yet not alone, for all around us were lovely cards of greetings.

I preach every Sunday 9.00 – 9.30 a.m. K. F. W.B. 980 (on deal). You are 8 hours ahead of us here. I must close. God bless you all richly.

Mrs. Nicholson joins me in much love to all and best wishes for 1952.

Yours as Ever
Wm. P. Nicholson Jn. 3.30.

Rev. Wm. P. Nicholson, 1950

1954

Belfast Telegraph – 15th March 1954

VETERAN ULSTER EVANGELIST IS OFF ON TOUR

Rev. W. P. Nicholson, the veteran Ulster evangelist, at the age of 78 has commenced a 3,000 miles preaching tour from California along the Pacific Coast to Vancouver, British Columbia.

The tour will last until the end of June, and then he will start on another in Florida, which is scheduled to last from August to December.

Mr. Nicholson, a man of strong personality with great strength of delivery, has conducted missions throughout the world.

During his tours of his native Ulster, halls were often packed to overflowing.

In Belfast on Saturday night a recording of a sermon preached by Mr. Nicholson was played back in Grove Baptist Church, Beersbridge Road, Belfast.

1956

Alliance News – 1956

SOME APPRECIATIONS OF HIS WORK IN IRELAND

I esteem it a great privilege and honour to be asked to write a short appreciation of Rev. William P. Nicholson on the occasion of his forthcoming 80th birthday, and of his work as an evangelist in Ireland during a very troublesome period in our island's history.

My first contact with Mr. Nicholson was when he came to Londonderry to conduct an Evangelistic Campaign in April, 1921. The late Mr. Charles Gordon was Secretary, Mr. R. D. Gordon, Chairman, the late Mr. John A. Pollock Treasurer, and the writer was Assistant Secretary.

I was not present at the opening meeting of the campaign in Clooney Hall on the first Sunday night, but was there the following Monday night, and when coming out from the prayer meeting he gave me a punch with his thumb on my tummy and said, "Say, Mr. Assistant Secretary, where were you last night?"

During that unforgettable mission, which lasted for about six weeks, the greater part of the time being in First Derry Presbyterian Church (when several hundred were led to the Lord Jesus Christ as Saviour and Friend, many of whom are still with us and witnessing to a good profession), a close bond of friendship and fellowship with the Missioner was formed, which has grown with the passing years. The late Mr. S. G. Montgomery (Bangor) was very fond of saying, "There was a man sent of God whose name was Willie P. Nicholson." At that time I thought it a bit strange, but on looking back through the years I am convinced of the truth of Mr. Montgomery's statement. Was ever a preacher so gifted and of so strong a personality, a man without fear or favour who exposed sin in all its ugliness and the ultimate eternal fate of the Christ rejector?

In his presentation of the Gospel he was unique in the manner in which he could present Christ in His saving power to the repentant sinner. Mr. Nicholson was and still is a fearless exposer of all modernistic soul destroying doctrine and preaching. The Gospel he proclaimed was full robed (if old fashioned); as the old Divines used to call it – the Gospel of the three R's – Ruination by the Fall, Redemption by the Shed Blood, Regeneration by the Holy Spirit.

The missions conducted by Mr. Nicholson throughout Northern Ireland were undoubted visitations from God and were characterized by the wide spiritual blessing. The Christian Church generally reaped the benefit by young men full of zeal entering the ministry and many others offering themselves for service in the foreign field. Travel where you will in Christian circles, it would be exceptional if you did not meet one of his spiritual children.

Perhaps the greatest testimony to the value and worth of his work is to be found in the Christian Workers' Unions which he inaugurated and which have not only preserved the fruits of the work but have continued to pursue the same aggressive evangelism, the deepening and upbuilding of the spiritual life of young converts, and seeking to interest them in foreign mission work.

Mr. Nicholson, during the past Autumn, undertook and finished an extended tour of 8,500 miles when he conducted Evangelistic Missions, also Bible readings to Christians in the Southern States of California with great blessing. May he yet be spared many days as an ambassador for the Lord.

J.G.

The Rev. William P. Nicholson is hoping to celebrate his 80th birthday in the Spring, and we congratulate him on having not only reached the allotted span, but having got well beyond it, thanks to the blessing of God and the care bestowed upon him by his beloved partner in life. It seems, therefore, a fitting time to refresh our memories by a brief appraisal of his work in Belfast.

Those of us who are old enough to cast our memory back thirty odd years can well remember the advent of "W. P." in our midst, and his impact on the religious life of the North of Ireland. Into a community that had experienced many movements of the Spirit of God, through various outstanding evangelists, came this – so it appeared to many – "stormy petrel" of evangelism, altogether different from his predecessors in his style, manner of speech, and presentation of the Gospel. Yes, William P. Nicholson was cast in a mould that was all his own.

By a certain section of the populace Mr. Nicholson was a much criticised man – he was crude, they said, when he spoke to ordinary men and women in a language they could understand. Of course, he said things that shocked the purists – he called a spade a spade. But everything "W. P." said and did was consecrated to the single purpose of bringing men and women to Christ. The success achieved in this respect confounded the critics and was undoubtedly an evidence of the seal of God upon his ministry.

There is no more touching scene in the Gospels than that depicted of the man who had lived amongst the tombs, battered and bruised by evil spirits, and who later was found sitting at the feet of the Master, clothed and in his right mind. This scene was duplicated again and again under the preaching of Mr. Nicholson, for a very considerable number of men and women who had for years been led captive by the devil at his will were, through the blessing of God and the evangelist's preaching, set gloriously free from the power and dominion of sin.

The success of any evangelistic mission is ultimately determined by the permanence of the work achieved, and judged by this standard, the missions of the Rev. Wm. P. Nicholson in Northern Ireland were an unqualified success. Even at this day (1956), after the passing of so many years, it is amazing the number of men and women we have still in our midst – they are to be found in all our mission halls and churches – who look back to the Nicholson missions as the time when they entered into an experience that transformed their whole lives. They were "born again" – and knew it – and the entire course of their lives had been changed.

In conclusion, may I say that while it was true of Mr. Nicholson as it was of his Master, that "the common people heard him gladly," these were not the only people who were reached; for besides that vast company, there are numerous men and women in every walk of life who ever since have been thanking God that, in His gracious providence, He sent the Rev. Wm. P. Nicholson to Northern Ireland.

HILLSBOROUGH C.W.U.
Letter from Rev. W. P. Nicholson

The Christian Workers Union, Hillsborough deputed Mr. H. Davis and Mr. J. McCandlis to write and felicitate the Rev. W. P. Nicholson on the occasion of his 80th birthday. The following reply was received from him.

Dear Friends,

Many, very many thanks for your kind letter, conveying the warm greetings from your C.W.U. members. It did me good and cheered me up, Strong paradox, while it humbled me, and it inspired me and encouraged me. My heart was strongly warmed and deeply stirred. Believe me, dear friends, my head wasn't swelled. Paul said, after years of sanctified, sacrificial living that he was "the least of all Saints". Some time after he said "he wasn't fit to be called a Saint". Almost at the end of his life he said, "He was the chief of sinners". Friends, we only grow, as we grow DOWN. We are born to be Crucified.

I will be 80 April 3rd (D.V.) I was Born Again May 22nd 1899. I was Spirit baptized and filled with the Spirit 7 months after. I have been preaching ever since, was ordained a Presbyterian Minister 1914. I have circled the globe over 12 times, and Glory to God it grows brighter and better every day. Jesus never fails, NEVER. We can never trust Him too much or ourselves too little; can we? I will be preaching every Sunday in April by Radio, reaching 1,000's unseen. Please pray for me. God richly bless you dear fellow warriors. May we never get used to men going to hell, but by all means save some. Much love (the real sort) to you all.

Maranatha! Hallelujah!

Yours restfully busy,
Wm. P. Nicholson Jno. 3.30

> ●
>
> I can do all things through Christ which strengtheneth me.   Phil. 4. 13
>
> ✳ ✳ ✳
>
> In His Strength -- I fight.
> In His Cause -- I work.
> In His Name -- I glory.
> Work the works of Him.
>
> ✳ ✳ ✳
>
> With best wishes for a Happy Christmas and all God's very best during 1957
>
> Rev. and Mrs. William P. Nicholson
> 1204 North Cedar Street
> Glendale 7. California. U. S. A.

CHRISTMAS CARD

1957

The Whig – 3rd April 1957

BANGOR-BORN U.S. RADIO EVANGELIST IS 81 TO-DAY

Celebrating to-day his 81st birthday at his home in California, U.S.A. is the Bangor-born evangelist, the Rev. William P. Nicholson, who was famed in Northern Ireland for his preaching abilities during the early 1920's.

Mr. Nicholson, who is still very active as an evangelist, conducted a 10-day campaign in America during January, and now preaches each Sunday over an American radio network.

During his life in Ireland he founded the Irish Alliance of Christian Workers' Unions the Hon. Secretary of which, Mr. T. McKibbin, Lisburn, received only a few days ago from him a letter inquiring about the work of the Alliance.

1958

Belfast Telegraph - 29th March 1958

BANGOR–BORN EVANGELIST IS RETURNING FROM U.S. FOR CAMPAIGN

One of Ulster's most forthright evangelists is returning from the United States in April for a six months' campaign. He is Rev. W. P. Nicholson, whose methods and results aroused considerable controversy nearly thirty years ago.

It was during the "troubles" and after working with the famous Chapman and Alexander team, that Mr. Nicholson started the revival campaign which left a permanent impression on the religious life of the country.

One of the organisers on that occasion was Mr. H. A. Johnston, a Belfast accountant, who recalled yesterday some of the highlights of the mission.

Shankhill Road Mission, West Belfast

At one series in the Shankhill Road Mission, he said, people coming by tram had to lie on the floorboards to avoid being hit by rifle bullets. Gunfire could be heard during the service.

He remembers too, the great crowd of shipyard workers surging round the Methodist Church on Newtownards Road. So great was the pressure that the railings collapsed.

Mr. Johnston agreed that to-day's generation would react differently to the methods of thirty years ago; but felt that the evangelist would be able to deal with the situation.

"After all, he has travelled the world seven times, has spoken to all types of people, and at 82 years has a wealth of experience" he said.

Belfast the most preached at city? "Maybe, but there are still plenty of young people on the streets any Sunday evening," said Mr. Johnston.

Discussing the outcome of the campaign, Rev. W. J. Carson, organising secretary of the C.E. movement in Ireland, said the movement was usually strengthened by successful missions like the Presbyterian one three years ago; but it was impossible to say what sort of reception Mr. Nicholson would get.

In No Doubt

Rev. G. E. Good, a Methodist City minister, said. "There is no doubt that 'W.P.' was a power thirty years ago and was the man for his day. Whether he will have such wide appeal today remains to be seen."

Certainly the local Committee organising his Belfast visit are in no doubt.

Their chairman, Mr. W. J. Morgan, said the present methods of evangelism were reaching church-going people, but there were many young folk completely outside the influence of the Church, and it was to them that the campaign would be directed.

Last word comes from Bangor-born Mr. Nicholson, who will spend his 82nd birthday in Ulster.

Writing to the committee, he says: "The doctor has seen me and passed me A.1. I feel fine, but I cannot do all I used to."

It is thus most unlikely that, like last time, his meetings will last from 6.30 –till 10.00 p.m.

The Northern Whig and Belfast Post – 21st April 1958

82 YEAR OLD NOTED EVANGELIST
RETURNS TO TOUR NATIVE ULSTER

Mr. W. P. Nicholson, 82 year old evangelist returned to his native Ulster yesterday for the first time in 10 years and was greeted as he stepped off the Liverpool boat by a deputation from the Irish Alliance of Christian Workers Unions – the movement which he founded 34 years ago.

A Bangor man, Mr. Nicholson who conducted memorable revival campaigns through the Province in the 1920s has been living in California, and after resting for a week in his home town he will begin a 6 month evangelical tour embracing the whole of Ulster.

Accompanied by his wife he was received at the quayside yesterday morning by Mr. H. Henderson, the Alliance President, Mr. W. J. Stafford, Vice President, Mr. Theo. McKibbin, Secretary, and numerous other friends.

Mr. Nicholson will hold his first meeting in Dromore, County Down, on Sunday, and will conclude his campaign with a monster meeting in Belfast in September.

Belfast Telegraph 22nd April 1958

"THROUGH RIFLE FIRE TO MISSION"
W. P. Nicholson – at 82 'Still a Rousing Speaker' - Recalls Past

The 82 year old evangelist threw back his head and laughed heartily. "Maybe I am not as young and as versatile as I used to be, but I can still preach a rousing sermon," he said.

In his old home in Princetown Road, Bangor, Rev. W. P. Nicholson, Ireland's most controversial preacher, who has just returned from California to conduct a six-month mission tour, reflected on his youth.

Twelve journeys around the world and many years living in America have done little to alter the rich Co. Down accent he acquired while a boy in Bangor. "Of course, I have had to take it a little easier since that heart attack about three years ago in Tasmania, but God has given me the strength, and here I am back in Ireland," he said.

He recalled making his first voyage as a very young cadet down Belfast Lough in the sailing ship Galgorm Castle; his shipwreck; his trip to Capetown in a badly damaged vessel.

"I wasn't cut out for the sea and, anyway, I detested the captain," he said.

He met an old schoolfriend Fred Orr, of Downpatrick, while at Capetown.

"Fred got me a job as a railway porter in Capetown, but this only lasted for a short time."

Before returning to Bangor "a little older and much richer in experience," Bill Nicholson had worked on the Cape to Cairo Railway as a fireman.

Tough Times

"They were very tough times," he said. "It was said that every railway sleeper on that line represented a white man's grave."

Proudly, "W.P.N." pointed out the exact place in the old home where, as he said, "while sitting by the fire with my mother and father on May 22, 1899, I made my decision for Christ."

Years working as a clerk with the Co. Down Railway followed before he went to Glasgow to study in the Bible Institution.

After graduating from this college he spent a number of years in evangelistic work in Scotland and England before going to America.

After the death of his father in 1921, Rev. W. P. Nicholson – by then he had been ordained into the Presbyterian Church in America – returned to Ireland for a mission that made his name a household word.

The campaign started in Portadown where, he said humorously, "we were very fortunate for there was a shortage of coal and the people of Portadown were kept warm in my mission hall."

"On to Lurgan, then Lisburn and Belfast. I will never forget the meetings on the Shankhill. It was during the time of the 'troubles' and people coming to the mission by tram had to lie flat in case they would be hit with rifle bullets.

Shoulder High

"Meetings in Ballymena cost me £70. More than 3,000 people flocked into the mission every night. There was so great a crush that they kept pushing each other out through the windows. The £70 had to be paid for new glass.

"On my last night in Ballymena, at nearly midnight," I was carried around the town shoulder high - it was a wonderful time.

"The campaign finished with a six-week mission in Londonderry which was most encouraging, to say the least of it."

"W.P.N." has been back in Ireland on a number of occasions since that campaign.

"My present trip is sponsored by a group of friends from Co. Fermanagh who sent the travel tickets for myself and my wife to my home in Glendale, California," he said.

"On this trip I only want to visit a number of branches of the Christian Workers' Unions, which I founded in Ireland following the first campaign."

"I do not want to draw people away from their own churches. The Christian Workers' Union was formed so that people from all denominations could join in worship, while still being good members of their own churches."

Mr. Nicholson will open his campaign in Dromore next Sunday and will speak also in Lisburn, Portadown, Garvagh, Omagh and Belfast. He will also visit Dublin and Glasgow.

Interior view of the Wellington Hall, Belfast

Belfast Telegraph 25th April 1958

THEY QUEUE FOR AN HOUR BEFORE PRAYER MEETING

People began queuing an hour before the start of the prayer service at which Rev. W. P. Nicholson well-known Ulster-born evangelist, spoke in the Wellington Hall, Belfast, last night.

Many of those who queued had to be turned away, and the Minor Hall of the Wellington Hall was filled to capacity for the meeting. About 80 per cent of those present were women.

Mr. Nicholson who is 82, is in Ulster for the first time in 10 years. He lives in Glendale, California, and has come here for the Ulster Evangelistic Campaign which is being held from May to September.

In his sermon, given with old type enthusiasm and well received, he urged people not to look on prayer as something "cissy". Prayer was needed by everybody, seven days a week, summer and winter, at home and abroad.

The Whig 25th April 1958

WORLD SINS DUE TO LACK OF PRAYER – NICHOLSON

"To be a praying man or a praying woman is the hardest thing in the world," the Rev. W. P. Nicholson, the famed evangelist, said at a united service of intercession in the Y.M.C.A. Minor Hall, Belfast last night.

Hell on Doorstep

Eight-two year old Mr. Nicholson, who is on a preaching tour of Ulster with his wife, displays energy and vitality in a remarkable manner for a man of his age.

"The minute that you become a praying man or woman," he said, "Hell is on your doorstep. And believe me, the Devil can be pretty stiff opposition as he has been at his job for the last 6,000 years."

Mr. Nicholson expressed the opinion that all the sins in the world to-day were due to "prayerlessness on the part of the Lord's people." The curse was that the work of the Lord was being laid upon the shoulders of so few.

Parents, he said, should give their children more chance of seeing them at prayer. "Let them see you kneeling at your beds at night, or even during the day, and let them hear you mention their names in your prayers. You have no idea how beneficial this will be to them in later life."

Doomed

He knew of many people, who, if caught kneeling at the foot of the bed praying, would jump to their feet with a guilty start and mumble that they were searching for something under the bed. "Never be ashamed to be caught praying," Mr. Nicholson said.

"And don't forget," he warned, "if you don't pray you are doomed. You can be baptised, vaccinated, immunized or anything else, but if you don't pray you will wake up in Hell."

Alliance News - 1958

MISSION REPORTS
LONDONDERRY

Memories came crowding back for a big section of the audience which gathered in Londonderry Guildhall for the service conducted by the well-known evangelist, the Rev. W. P. Nicholson – memories of his visit in the 1920's when a wave of religious enthusiasm swept through the city and made Mr. Nicholson the most talked of evangelist in his generation.

He last preached in Derry in 1948, and when he sailed from his native Ulster to return to America, having passed three score and ten, it was not anticipated that he would ever come to Ireland to preach again.

Always a man of remarkable vitality, as those who heard him over thirty years ago will remember, he has still enough of the old fire and spirit left to belie his advancing years. He has now passed his 82nd birthday, a veteran in active service, but he was not long "on the bridge" until all the well-known features of a Nicholson meeting were in evidence.

He has not yet reached the stage where he is content simply to preach. Once he took over the meeting he soon had the audience singing lustily at the same familiar choruses, and he showed his old love for the unusual by having the men and women whistle in turn.

On the opening night he gave a typical hard-hitting address on the necessity of the New Birth.

Mr. Nicholson prefaced his address by saying he never thought he would see Ireland again. He had been told his days were numbered and his preaching over. "After a rest I was able to go at it again. When I was invited back to Ulster I was a bit hesitant, but when I mentioned the matter to my wife the bags were packed and off we started again."

"I think," he said wistfully, "this is the last time unless the Lord makes me a centenarian."

At 82, he said he was not able to do very much and he was acting on doctor's orders by curtailing his missions to a week at a time, which was something new for him.

The services continued in the Carlisle Road Presbyterian Church and there were large attendances and evident blessing. The Mission concluded on the following Sunday in the Guildhall which was packed to capacity.

In presiding, Mr. T. S. Mooney said that it was a time of gladness and sadness – 'Gladness because it has been a very happy, pleasant and profitable week, and sadness because we feel it might possibly be the last occasion we are likely to have Mr. Nicholson with us. Here in the Maiden City his name is honoured and beloved. He has been prayed for these past 35 years. He has many friends who have remembered him and who will remember him as long as they live."

LISBURN

Market Street, Lisburn.
The CWU Hall is the white building on the left.

The Mission in the C.W.U. Hall, Lisburn, from 4th – 11th May 1958, was a time of rich blessing. Much prayer had gone up beforehand, and there was a real spirit of expectancy by many who knew Mr. Nicholson and by the younger generation who were eager to hear him. Then what seemed disappointment was turned into real blessing. Mr. Nicholson took ill and for the first three days Mr. William Wylie, General Secretary of the Belfast City Mission, had to step into the breach. This was the Lord's doing, and the crowds who heard Mr. Wylie were not disappointed. He preached with great power, and when Mr. Nicholson was fully restored, it was evident the Lord had already begun to work.

Mr. Nicholson spoke mostly to Christians, and these were days of heart-searching. Many came forward as a token that they were surrendering their lives to God. The crowds were so great that the meetings always commenced half an hour before the advertised time. On Sundays the hall was packed fully an hour before the start of the service.

The singing of the old Gospel hymns was a tonic. Mr. T. McKibbin conducted the community singing and also presided at the services. Mrs. H. Sloan was the pianist.

Mr. Theo McKibbin who served for many years as Secretary of Lisburn C.W.U. and as General Secretary of the Irish Alliance of Christian Workers' Unions.

Belfast Telegraph 12th May 1958

BELFAST WELCOME FOR REV. W. P. NICHOLSON

The Wellington Hall, Belfast, was crowded for the welcome to Rev. W. P. and Mrs. Nicholson. The proceedings were relayed by microphone to the Minor Hall which was also filled.

Mr. W. J. Stafford (Dromara), who presided, spoke of the success of the early missions conducted by Mr. Nicholson in 1921-1923.

Mr. Nicholson said that in his early life, he was greatly helped by the Bangor Christian Workers' Society, in the founding of which the late Dr. Henry Montgomery took a leading part. It was due to that influence that after the campaigns of the twenties he encouraged the formation of Christian Workers' Unions.

GARVAGH C.W.U. MISSION – 18th – 25th May 1958

Garvagh C.W.U. Minutes record:

"Reports were given on Rev. W. P. Nicholson's Campaign which showed that God's hand had been upon his servant and that the seal of God's approval had been upon this effort in Garvagh."

Belfast Telegraph 14th June 1958

ERADICATE GRUDGES, CALL BY MINISTER

Grudges in the hearts of the people are keeping back a much needed religious revival.

This view was expressed by Rev. W. P. Nicholson in Belfast Y.M.C.A. Minor Hall last night.

Mr. Nicholson, who is holding a series of meetings in connection with his Belfast campaign, said grudges among individuals and nations are frustrating God's aspirations.

"People must realise that where there is bitterness God cannot solve our differences and problems," he declared. "If we don't forgive our brother God cannot forgive us."

There was a great deal of prayer these days. But it had not quality.

'No Time'

"If we pray to God we must do so penitently and humbly, but we must not try to bargain with our Maker," Mr. Nicholson continued.

"The trouble with many is that they have not the time to pray. If you cannot find the time you have got to make it."

Mr. Nicholson added that all promises of God were conditional.

"He cannot grant forgiveness unless the believer has already forgiven beforehand," he said.

"Grudges are held even by the most devout Christians, many not realising that belief is not enough."

Mr. Nicholson said it was his hope that during the campaign there would be a wholesale wiping out of grudges, so that God would have a clear field on which to act.

Mr. W. J. Morgan presided.

Portrush Presbyterian Church

Belfast Telegraph 9th August 1958

EVANGELIST W. P. NICHOLSON AT PORTRUSH

The veteran Ulster-born evangelist, 82 year old Rev. W. P. Nicholson, will enter another stage of a strenuous six-month campaign when he addresses a Convention at Portrush tomorrow.

Mr. Nicholson will be the main speaker at the Convention in the Presbyterian Church there, which will last for a week.

Since he arrived in Ulster from his home in Glendale, California, four months ago, he has carried out a heavy programme of engagements.

Missions have been conducted at Dromore, Lisburn, Garvagh, Londonderry, Ballymena, and Enniskillen.

When the Portrush Convention ends – all Mr. Nicholson's meetings are sponsored by the Irish Alliance of Christian Workers' Unions – he will travel to Glasgow for a short campaign. Then he will go to the Ulster Hall, and finally to the Y.M.C.A. in Dublin.

A farewell meeting will be held in Belfast Y.M.C.A. Immediately he arrives back in the U.S., he will appear on TV. He also conducts a weekly radio programme there.

To-day, Mr. Nicholson, who has travelled 12 times round the world, spent the day at the home of a friend, Mr. Thomas Thompson, of Garvagh. Mr. Thompson presented him with a new car for his tour.

Mr. Nicholson is staying with his brother-in-law, Dr. J. B. Hanna, at Princetown Road, Bangor.

Belfast Telegraph 13th September 1958

EVANGELIST HAS TO POSTPONE BELFAST MISSION

On medical advice Rev. W. P. Nicholson, the 82 year old Ulster born evangelist has been forced to postpone his Belfast mission, due to open on Sunday week.

For the past week has been undergoing treatment in Bangor Hospital but it is expected that he will leave hospital in a few days.

His campaign in Belfast was due to open in the Ulster Hall and would have been similar to that held by him in the city more than 25 years ago.

Mr. Nicholson was to have taken part in a campaign in Glasgow this week and was due to conduct a campaign in Dublin at the beginning of next month, but his doctors have advised him not to undertake a full-scale campaign.

Belfast Telegraph 18th September 1958

EVANGELIST IS 'COMFORTABLE'

Rev. W. P. Nicholson, the 82 year old Ulster-born evangelist, who is in Bangor Hospital, was stated to-day to be "fairly comfortable."

Mr. Nicholson was due to start a campaign in Belfast on Sunday, but has been forced to postpone it on medical advice. He also intended to conduct a campaign in Dublin at the beginning of next month.

Mr. Nicholson hopes to leave hospital shortly, but no definite date has been fixed for his discharge.

Belfast Telegraph – 10th October 1958

EVANGELIST IS TO PREACH AGAIN

Rev. W. P. Nicholson who has been ill for the past six weeks, has now completely recovered and is to start a mission in the King's Hall, Bangor, on Sunday, October 16th which he hopes to continue until November 2nd.

The farewell meeting arranged by the Irish Alliance of Christian Workers, which had to be cancelled, will take place on Wednesday, November 12th, in the Wellington Hall, Belfast.

Mr. and Mrs. Nicholson sail from Belfast on November 21st via Liverpool for their home in Glendale, California.

Belfast Telegraph - 27th October 1958

IMPORTANCE OF PRAYER STRESSED BY MINISTER

Many people were unable to gain admittance to the King's Hall, Bangor, last night, when Rev. W. P. Nicholson, 82 year old evangelist, began a week's mission.

Since leaving his native Bangor for the United States he has preached in nearly every country in the world. The importance of prayer was the theme for Mr. Nicholson's address last night. He regretted the fact that prayer meetings were no longer popular and said that at a Presbyterian church in Ballymena they no longer held prayer meetings, but a meditation.

He wondered what people would say if they arrived home from work for a meal and were told that they would have a meditation instead.

Mr. C. G. Flannigan, Hon. Secretary of Bangor Christian Workers' Society, presided. Arrangements have been made to relay to-night's meeting to the minor hall.

Belfast Telegraph – 11th November 1958

EVANGELIST'S LAST SERMON HERE

Rev. W. P. Nicholson, the evangelist, will preach the farewell sermon of his present mission in the Wellington Hall tomorrow evening.

It is likely to be the last occasion he will preach in Belfast as he is now in his 83rd year.

Shipyard men and aircraft workers will march from the Coalmen's Hall, Donegall Quay, to take part.

Belfast Telegraph – 13th November 1958

FAREWELL SERVICE FOR REV. W. P. NICHOLSON

The Wellington Hall, Belfast, was filled last night when a farewell service was held for Rev. W. P. Nicholson, the veteran missionary, who is leaving Northern Ireland on November 21 to return to America.

The hall can hold about 1,800 people. Many were unable to gain admission.

Mr. Nicholson said that it was rather queer to feel he would never see those present again in this life.

Farewell greetings to Mr. and Mrs. Nicholson were conveyed by Mr. T. Johnston, one of the oldest workers of the Irish Alliance of Christian Workers' Unions, the organisers of the meeting.

Before the service 500 people, including workers from the shipbuilding and aircraft industries, marched to the Wellington Hall from the Coalmen's Mission at the Queen's Quay, under the leadership of Mr. S. Spence. They were headed by the Belfast Christian Accordion Band

Belfast Telegraph - 17th November 1958

NOTED EVANGELIST VISITS GARVAGH

Rev. W. P. Nicholson, the noted Irish evangelist, delivered his last address in the Presbyterian Hall, Garvagh, last night, before returning to the U.S.A. next week.

Mr. T. B. F. Thompson, Garvagh, President of Garvagh Christian Workers' Union, who sponsored the meeting presided.

Mr. Nicholson, he said, had travelled the world and had preached in many great cities, yet he had come back to his native Ulster to finish his campaign.

Mr. Thompson extended good wishes to Rev. and Mrs. Nicholson.

Rev. & Mrs. W. P. Nicholson with their dog 'Brutus'
The last photograph taken at Garvagh 1958

1959

Belfast Telegraph – 12th September 1959

REV. NICHOLSON TO SETTLE IN ULSTER

Rev. W. P. Nicholson, the Ulster born evangelist and Mrs. Nicholson are returning to the Province and plan to settle down in Bangor, it is learned to-day.

They are sailing from New York on October 9th and are due in Belfast on October 18th.

Mr. Nicholson will later visit Switzerland for heart treatment.

The trans Atlantic liner 'Mauritania' on which the Nicholsons were travelling home

Courtesy of Harland & Wolff

Belfast Telegraph – 23rd October 1959

REV. W. P. NICHOLSON ILL IN CORK HOSPITAL
ULSTER EVANGELIST 'CRITICAL'

Rev. W. P. Nicholson the celebrated Ulster evangelist, is "very critically ill" in a Cork hospital.

Mr. Nicholson was taken from the trans-Atlantic liner 'Mauritania' when she called at Cork on the way to Liverpool.

His wife is maintaining a day and night vigil at his bedside. They were coming to settle in Bangor.

Mr. Nicholson, who is 83, has been suffering from heart trouble for some time. Complications arose and he collapsed on the voyage.

He was taken ashore by stretcher to the Victoria Hospital, where he is still unconscious.

Mrs. Nicholson said to-day, "I am hoping and hoping that I may be able to have him brought to Belfast by ambulance.

"But he is not well enough to be moved, and I haven't been able to make any arrangements."

Improved

"They said he had improved a bit yesterday, but he had a very bad night, and to-day he is still very critically ill. I am not leaving his bedside."

Mr. Nicholson, a Presbyterian minister who was once a railway clerk, became a household name in Ulster during the 1920's for his forthright brand of evangelism.

He spent many years in Glendale, California, but returned home last year to conduct another Ulster campaign.

Before he could do so, however, he was admitted to Bangor hospital for treatment, and doctors advised him not to go through with a full-scale campaign. But he addressed several meetings before returning to America.

Mr. Nicholson planned to go to Switzerland for heart treatment after he came home.

When he was here last year he stayed with his brother-in-law, Dr. J. B. Hanna, at Princetown Road, Bangor.

Belfast Newsletter

HOME CALL – OCTOBER 29th 1959

NICHOLSON – October 29, 1959, at Victoria Hospital, Cork, the Rev. William P., beloved husband of Fanny Elizabeth Nicholson. Funeral to-day (Monday), November 2. Service 2.30 p.m. at Hamilton Road Presbyterian Church, Bangor, thence to Clandeboye Cemetery. (No flowers, by request - instead, money sent to evangelical Missions). Redeemed by His precious blood.

The Whig- Friday, 30th October 1959

THE REV. W. P. NICHOLSON DIES IN CORK

The death took place last night in the Victoria Hospital, Cork, of the Rev. W. P. Nicholson, the veteran Ulster-born evangelist, who, during 50 years had conducted revival campaigns in many parts of the world. He was 83.

County Down Spectator – 6th November 1959

DEATH OF REV. W. P. NICHOLSON
Over 1,000 at funeral service

Rev. William Patteson Nicholson, who died in Victoria Hospital, Cork, on Thursday of last week, has left an indelible mark in various parts of the world. News of the eighty-three-year old evangelist's death was received with particular regret in his native Bangor, and the fact that Hamilton Road Presbyterian church was filled by over 1,000 people for the funeral service on Monday bore striking testimony of his work and worth.

As Mr. Nicholson would have wished, the service was one of praise and thanksgiving – thanksgiving to God for a servant who helped the people of his own land at a critical stage in their history and the people of many other countries.

Mr. Nicholson was a son of the late Captain and Mrs. John Nicholson, of Ellenville, Princetown Road, Bangor – the house now occupied by Dr. J. B. Hanna, deceased's brother-in-law. He worshipped in Trinity Presbyterian Church, and later the family was also connected with Hamilton Road Presbyterian.

Ordained in America

He spent some years at sea and as a clerk with the County Down Railway before he went to Glasgow to study in the Bible Institute. After graduating from this college he spent a number of years in evangelistic work in Scotland and England before going to America. He was ordained in the Presbyterian Church of America before returning to Ireland to conduct a mission that made his name a household word.

It was during the "troubles" some thirty-five years ago, and after working with the famous Chapman and Alexander team, that Mr. Nicholson started his historical campaign. At one series in the Shankhill Road Mission people coming by tram had to lie on the floorboards to avoid being hit by rifle bullets. Gunfire could be heard during the service. On another occasion a crowd of shipyard workers surged round the Methodist Church on Newtownards Road, Belfast, and so great was the pressure that the railings collapsed.

Mr. Nicholson founded the Christian Workers' Union at this time.

He returned to his home in Glendale, California, and for many years broadcast regularly from Los Angeles. He re-visited Ulster ten years ago, and in 1954 at the age of 78 – he made a 3,000 miles preaching tour of the Pacific Coast from California to Vancouver, following this up with another extended campaign in Florida.

Last Ulster Campaign

Mr. Nicholson returned to Ulster in April of last year to conduct a campaign which was to take him to Lisburn, Portadown, Garvagh, Omagh and Belfast, as well as Dublin and Glasgow, but before this ambitious programme was completed he became seriously ill. He had accepted an invitation to speak at the 1958 Worldwide Missionary Convention in Bangor, but during the week of the Convention he was in Bangor Hospital. He made a miraculous recovery, and before leaving for the States in October last he conducted a week's mission in the King's Hall, Bangor, under the auspices of Bangor Christian Workers' Society. Each night the hall was filled to capacity, and Mr. Nicholson spoke with his old vigour and fervour. He stressed the importance and power of prayer, exhorting his hearers to pray several times a day at their work bench, office desk, at the wheel of a car or in whatever circumstances they found themselves. As in his earlier and larger missions, many were helped by his practical preaching.

Mr. Nicholson was an outstanding personality both in and out of the pulpit. He possessed a rich sense of humour and a deep understanding of the problems confronting his fellowmen. He was very much a "man's man" – a fact that was evident in the very large proportion of men who stayed away from business to attend the funeral service. From Newtownards, Lisburn, Belfast and many other centres they came – to pay their last tribute to an inspired man who had changed the lives of many.

It was appropriate that at the funeral service the pulpit of Hamilton Road Presbyterian Church was occupied by representatives of various denominations and religious societies. Rev. D. Burke, B.A., minister of the congregation, announced that it was the wish of Mr. Nicholson that the service should be happy and that there might be much singing.

The hymns chosen were among his favourites – "The Lord's my Shepherd," "How Sweet the Name of Jesus Sounds," "There is a Fountain filled with Blood," and "For all the Saints." Members of the Irish Alliance of Christian Workers' Unions occupied the choir seats, and Mr. James Caswell was at the organ.

Mr. Burke was accompanied in the pulpit by Mr. Matt Boland (I.A.C.W.U.) Rev. John T. Carson, B.A. (Trinity Presbyterian Church), Rev. James Dunlop, M.A. (Oldpark Presbyterian Church), Mr. R. Frazer (Faith Mission) and Mr. William Wylie (B.C.M.)

Hamilton Road Presbyterian Church, Bangor

Alliance News – January – March 1960

HOMECALL OF REV. WM. P. NICHOLSON
Funeral Service

The funeral took place from Hamilton Road Presbyterian Church, Bangor, at 2 p.m. on Monday, 2nd November, when a company of over a thousand gathered to pay their last tribute to one who had been the instrument through whom blessing had been brought to many in the past generation.

The service in the church was conducted by the minister, Rev. David Burke, and opened with the 23rd Psalm, followed by prayer. The second hymn was John Newton's "How sweet the Name of Jesus Sounds" and Mr. Noel Grant read the Scriptures.

After the singing of Wm. Cowper's hymn "There is a fountain filled with Blood" the Rev. James Dunlop (Oldpark Presbyterian Church) gave the following address:

"Our friend, and stalwart in the faith W. P. Nicholson has gone from us. In such an hour as this, our hearts are hushed, our thoughts arrested, our memories stirred, and our sympathies quickened; as we seek to grasp and realise something of what he meant to his generation, and to the cause of Christ which he espoused and defended and proclaimed; he who now is no more, as far as this world is concerned.

We do not meet in this place just to praise famous men; we are not here, nor is this the time, to utter panegyrics concerning Mr. Nicholson; but we solemnly vow to give thanks to God for this child and servant of His, and for what He enabled him to be and to do during his span on earth.

Arrested in his young manhood by Christ Himself, and raised by Him from a life of sin and dissoluteness to an experience of Divine grace and cleansing and power, William Nicholson became possessed of a surpassing love for the Gospel and a passion to win souls to a similar experience of salvation. This love and passion never wavered throughout his life. To him to live was Christ. He could never be other than an evangelist. The calling that was laid upon him brought its joys and its tribulations, its rewards and its deprivations; but under the constraint of Christ, he could be and could accept no other and, as he laid his gifts, his personality, his fervour, on the altar for Christ, how graciously God took them and used them for His purposes! Here was a man, rugged in word and character, yet very human endowed with rich humour; a man strong in conviction, fearless and uncompromising towards anything which he considered would turn him from the path of his heavenly duty, impatient of anything that to him savoured of cant and hypocrisy; and upon such a man God laid His hand in a unique way.

In many places over the world, in spheres high and low, he became a blessing to his fellowmen; and we here in his native Ulster are not likely for a long time to forget how mightily God chose to work through him in the early 1920's especially. We all know that he became in some respects a controversial figure; oftentimes, in his zeal, he brought not peace on the earth, but a sword, like his Lord; but none could deny his passion for the Gospel, nor the power with which he presented it to men. I have never known such a preacher of the Gospel as the Rev. W. P. Nicholson; I have never known one who, under God, made such an appeal to men particularly, in their own language. Here was one whom God was pleased to raise up at a critical time in the history of our Province, to call people from sin and civil strife to repentance and faith towards Jesus Christ; one who, in a remarkable degree, was given the ear of the people; and one who was the instrument of leading hundreds of individuals into a vital, regenerating experience of God's grace in Christ, so that their lives were transformed. And that movement of God, and its impetus on the work of God in this and other lands, remain to this day.

Our praise at this service is, not to the man, but to the power of God in and through him. As he now stands before the Throne in his Lord's Presence we would re-echo the cry: "Not unto us, not unto us, O Lord, but unto Thy Name be glory!" His earthly motto was, "He must increase and I must decrease"; and now "the Lamb must have all the glory in Emmanuel's Land." But we give thanks for him, and we feel the constraint of his unfaltering devotion to spend our strength and wear out our days in the service of the same Lord and Saviour, which is the one thing that matters in the last resort.

I have been asking myself, if it were possible for him, whose voice is now silent, and whose earthly body we are now to lay to rest – if it were possible for him to speak, what would he say? What would he want anyone to say at this time? Of one thing I am sure – he would not want attention drawn to himself that should be given to Jesus Christ. And he would be especially concerned that all present on an occasion like this really knew his Saviour. I would not be true to his memory and his spirit, therefore, if I did not lovingly and earnestly remind every individual here of the truth of the central message that he proclaimed, that each must accept Christ as Saviour to have the life that is eternal. In the hour of the passing of death, when we are face to face with eternal issues, and when in our hearts we acknowledge our only hope to be in the Christ of the gospel, it is surely fitting that we should all make sure of our part in Him. There is no other way of life, here or hereafter. So, Mr. Nicholson, being dead, would yet speak.

He is gone from us, yet, just a little before us. But he is not dead he is alive. The trumpets have sounded for him on the other side. And what a host have greeted and will greet him over there, to whom, as to so many of us here, he was the very savour of life! The triumphant Christian assurance, which he reiterated again and again, of the life beyond with Christ, which is far better, is now a reality to him; and, behold, the half had not been told!

Truly, in time of parting and sorrow like this, we who are Christ's do not "sorrow as those who have no hope, but rather as those who have been brought again to a living hope through Him and His resurrection from the dead." For "death is swallowed up in victory." And "blessed are the dead which die in the Lord from henceforth, that they may rest from their labours; and their works do follow them."

To Mrs. Nicholson, bereft of her partner in life, we tender our deep and sincere sympathy. All that I have said about him she has known in a more intimate way than any. She has shared his joys and his tribulations; she has known that personal graciousness that his close friends knew in fellowship with him, that deep appreciation he had of friendliness and kindness; but more, she has been his life and sustainer for many years. Lovingly we would say to her, as he would, that the bonds that are in Christ are never severed, and as even now she shares in his triumph by faith, and looks forward to the day of glad re-union in Glory, so the living Christ will be all to her for the rest of the journey. May the assurance of His all-sufficient strength, and the peace of God that passeth all understanding, be her abiding portion!

As for us all, let the eternal realities become more vivid to us and more compelling in our lives. Let us, like every true servant of God, live for the eternal values, and sit lightly by the things of time and sense. For what else matters in the end?

So we take leave of W. P. Nicholson, until the morning, and as we think of his influence on earth in his time, and consider the times in which we now live, we are constrained to cry:

> God give us men! A time like this demands
> Strong men, great hearts, true faith and ready hands.
> Men whom the spoils of office cannot buy
> Men who possess opinions and a will,
> Men who have honour – men who will not lie,
> Men who can stand before a demagogue and
> Storm his treacherous flatteries without winking;
> Tall men! Sun-crowed, who live above the fog
> In public duty, and in private thinking.
> God give us men!

Prayer was offered by the Rev. John T. Carson (Trinity Presbyterian Church, Bangor) and the service concluded with the singing of the triumphant hymn "For all the saints, who from their labours rest."

County Down Spectator – 6th November 1959

The mourners included Mr. Nicholson's widow, his sister-in-law, Miss Jennie Hanna; his brother-in-law, Dr. J. B. Hanna; and Dr. H. H. Collier and Mr. George F. C. Balmer, who are married to nieces of Mr. Nicholson.

One large floral tribute covered the coffin, by 'special request' the money which would have been spent on wreaths has been sent to evangelistic missions.

Crowds gathered in Hamilton Road and Main Street as the cortege proceeded to Clandeboye Cemetery. Blinds were drawn along the route. Immediately behind the coffin walked Dr. Hanna, Dr. Collier and Mr. Balmer.

The service at the graveside was conducted by Rev. J. T. Carson, B.A.

The funeral cortege of Rev. Wm. P. Nicholson
on the way to Clandeboye Cemetery

(Alliance News   January - March 1960)

Graveside Service

A large gathering gathered in the new Clandeboye Cemetery when the Rev. David Burke opened the graveside service. The much loved hymn "There is a fountain filled with blood" was sung with fervour after which Mr. R. Frazer (Faith Mission) read the Scripture. The Rev. James Wiseheart, in the course of a short address said that he wished to pay the tribute of a son in the faith to Mr. Nicholson. He was brought to a knowledge of Jesus Christ as Saviour on the 21st September, 1922, in the mission held in The Cripples' Institute (Donegall Road). Little did he think then of the possibility of his entering the Christian ministry or of being called upon to pay a last tribute to the life and memory of W. P. Nicholson.

Paul's counsel to Timothy "Do the work of an Evangelist" characterised the life of their departed brother. He pursued this one task with fidelity and with his whole heart. The Gospel which he preached was a challenge to men. He was in every sense a man's man. He challenged the minds of men and appealed to their hearts. His message was one of joy – the joy of sins forgiven – with the burden like that of

Bunyan's Pilgrim rolled away. He preached a Gospel of full salvation. Like Paul he fought a good fight, and finished his course and kept the faith. There was only one W. P. Nicholson and they thanked God for him. All over the world there were ministers, missionaries and others who thanked God for every remembrance of their departed friend.

The committal service was offered by the Rev. John T. Carson and prayer was offered by Pastor Wm. Weir (Grove Baptist Church, Belfast) and by Mr. Wm. Wylie (Belfast City Mission).

County Down Spectator – 6th November 1959

BAPTIST UNION'S TRIBUTE

When the news of the death of the Rev. W. P. Nicholson reached the Baptist Union of Ireland while it was in session in Belfast, the meeting was adjourned to enable a resolution of sympathy with Mrs. Nicholson to be passed.

The President and Secretary attended the funeral officially to represent Irish Baptists.

AT ASSEMBLY HALL SERVICE

Preaching in the Assembly Hall service on Sunday the Rev. Rupert Gibson, Superintendent of the Irish Mission of the Presbyterian Church referred to the passing of the Rev. W. P. Nicholson.

Mr Gibson said that Mr. Nicholson had been a sincere and forceful speaker who had exercised a very useful ministry. He had a wonderful gift of being able to reach many who might otherwise not have been touched by the gospel.

From: W.P. Nicholson – Flame for God in Ulster
by S. W. Murray

In a tribute, the Editor of Bright Words (Faith Mission magazine) said:
"We mourn the passing of a great man who was fearless in his denunciation of sin, had a wonderful love for the Lord, and a great passion for souls. As a man he was extremely loveable and had a keen sense of humour. A favourite verse of his was the following:

E're since by faith I saw the stream
Thy flowing wounds supply,
Redeeming love has been my theme
And shall be till I die.

This was his testimony to the last, even during his time in hospital when he was semi-conscious, until the Lord took him home a tired and happy warrior.

Belfast Newsletter – 10th November, 1959

MEMORIAL SERVICE TO THE REV. W. P. NICHOLSON AT WELLINGTON HALL

No man ever made such a mark on the religious life in Northern Ireland as that made by Rev. W. P. Nicholson. He was one of the greatest preachers.

These were among the tributes paid to Mr. Nicholson at a memorial service in the Wellington Hall, Belfast, last night.

The Rev. James Dunlop said that Mr. Nicholson was a man loved by all who had ever come into contact with him. "He spoke to the people in their own language," said Mr. Dunlop, "and his robust style and humour attracted his listeners from the very beginning. Well it was for Ulster that such a man came at that critical time in her history 40 years ago, when he called the country's manhood from sin and civil strife to the knowledge of Jesus Christ."

It was not an occasion for sorrow or mourning, Mr. Dunlop went on, but an occasion for joy. "It would not be Mr. Nicholson's wish that we should meet here to mourn his passing," he said, "but that we should rejoice that he is with the Lord."

Those who paid tributes to Mr. Nicholson included Mr. R. Frazer, Faith Mission, Mr. T. Johnstone, Christian Workers Union, Mr. R. Brown, Christian Endeavour, Mr. Wylie, Belfast City Mission, Pastor W. Wilson, Baptist Church, and Mr. J. Rennie Thompson.

Others taking part included Mr. J. Cochrane, Y.M.C.A. Evangelist, Dublin, Mrs. T. McKibbin, who sang a solo, and the Rev. W. J. Grier, Irish Evangelical Church.

The Leader - November 1959

MEMORIAL SERVICE – BALLYNAHINCH

The death of the great Ulster evangelist, the Rev. W. P. Nicholson, was recalled in The Leader during November 1959. The paper reported on a memorial service held for W.P., who had founded the Christian Workers' Union movement.

The service, held in Ballynahinch, was conducted by Mr. Edwin Patterson, one of the oldest members of the Union in the town and an intimate friend of Mr. Nicholson.

Nicholson had first held a mission in Ballynahinch in 1925. Mr. Patterson announced the opening hymn, 'How sweet the name of Jesus Sounds' sung to the Salvation Army tune. It had been a great favourite of the evangelist.

Mr. William P. Moore led the opening prayer and Mr. George Cowan, Lisburn, sang the solo, 'There is singing up in Heaven.'

Mr. Andy Maze gave a personal testimony, relating how he first went to hear Nicholson preach in Lisburn in 1922. After several visits he became personally interested until the night of his conversion.

Mr. Maze paid tribute to the fearless and forthright preaching of the great evangelist.

There was a further solo from Mr. Cowan 'Is your all on the Altar of Sacrifice laid?' and the singing of another favourite hymn,' I was once far away from the Saviour'.

Mr. William Wylie of the City Mission told how he had been converted under the preaching of the Rev. W. P. Nicholson in Wellington Street Presbyterian Church, Ballymena. It happened in 1923 and was a memory of the evangelist he was not likely to forget.

Memory

The second memory was in 1936 when, on a Sunday afternoon, Mr. Nicholson was to commence a mission in Ballynahinch. "I received a telephone message that Mr. Nicholson had been in an accident in Derry and asking me to deputise." Mr. Wylie recalled it was with fear and trembling he made his way into the bedroom of Nicholson. "He asked me to fish for souls."

Mr. Wylie said this was typical of the man, although in intense pain the thoughts of his work as an evangelist were still uppermost in his mind.

The third memory was of a farewell meeting in the Wellington Hall, Belfast, when the veteran evangelist clasped his hand and thanked him for assisting at the various meetings. Mr. Wylie appealed for the wholehearted re-dedication of lives on the part of all Christians. It was the only hope of the hour.

'Everyone a Soul Winner' was the theme of the service and it was a touching scene to see so many on their feet as an indication of their full surrender to the Lord.

It was a fitting tribute to the memory of the greatest evangelist of our time.

Headstone of Rev. W. P. Nicholson in
Clandeboye Cemetery,Bangor

As used in the 1859 Revival.

Nicholson United Mission

MY DECISION

I take God the Father to be my God, *(1 Thess. i, 9).*

I take God the Son to be my Saviour, *(Acts v, 31).*

I take God the Holy Ghost to be my Sanctifier, *(1 Peter i, 2).*

I take the Word of God to be my Rule, *(2 Tim. iii, 16-17).*

I take the People of God to be my People, *(Ruth i, 16-17).*

I likewise dedicate myself wholly to the Lord, *(Rom. xiv, 7-8)*

And I do this prayerfully, (Psalm cxix, 94) : deliberately, *(Joshua xxiv, 15)* : sincerely, *(2 Cor. i, 12)* : freely, *(Psalm cx, 3)* : and for ever, (Rom. viii, 35-39).

Signed, _____

Date, _____

TO GOD BE THE GLORY

—- oOo —-

'Not unto us, O Lord, Not unto us,
but unto thy name give glory.'
Psalm 115 v.1a.

The bullets flew and people died,
As Ulster in the twenties cried
For peace and calm from all unrest,
A peace that would withstand each test.

Through strife did reign and times confuse,
God sent a man to bring Good News,
A forthright man from County Down
He 'sowed the seed' in every town.

He cared not for the world's acclaim
To bring God's message was his aim.
The Holy Spirit fell in power,
He was God's man for Ulster's hour.

W. P. Nicholson was his name
And to his meetings thousands came.
The Gospel message was received
And many on the Lord believed.

Revival blessing touched our land
As churches filled 'No room to stand',
With humour He did preach the Word,
But people heard the voice of God.

From such beginnings came the plan
For mission halls throughout the land.
Halls of hope, with teaching clear,
Who welcomed all, 'No labels here.'

The 'Irish Alliance' was begun
The vision of Mr. Nicholson.
Its aim to nurture converts new,
And others find the Saviour too.

To spread the Word in printed form
The first 'Alliance News' was born,
A beacon of light proclaiming God's power.
A witness to many near and far.

The years passed by, with progress made,
As missions in every hall were held.
The 'C.W.U.' was the place to go,
A 'taste of Heaven' here below.

Lisburn, Dromore and Ballyclare,
Garvagh, Coleraine, Bangor fair,
Strabane and Cookstown, Portadown,
A hall in nearly every town.

Then in the year of 'thirty-five'
Portrush Convention became alive.
Speakers and singers of great renown
Brought thousands to this seaside town.

Evangelists on the scene did come
William Millar was number one.
Many more to follow on,
Wheeler, Boland, Grant and Dunn.

Finlay, McCracken, Creagmile too,
Pickering, Black and Cregan who
All proclaimed God's Saving Grace;
And many found in Heaven a place.

The years have passed since 'W.P.'
Began His work last century
He now has gone to his reward
But Ireland still needs Christ the Lord.

So Christians let us carry on
The work of Mr. Nicholson,
With thousands on the road to Hell
The Gospel Message we must tell.

For God is still the same today,
His power is able, come what may,
Once more we need His mighty Hand,
His Spirit poured upon our land.

O rend the Heavens Lord we pray
Baptise us with Thy fire today
Sweep through our land with power divine
And send Revival in our time.

Mavis Heane

Meet Me There

Meet me there! Oh, meet me there!
In the Heavenly world so fair,
Where our Lord has entered in,
And where comes no taint of sin;
And our friends of long ago,
Clad in raiment white as snow,
Such as all the ransomed wear -
Meet me there! yes - meet me there!

Meet me there! Oh, meet me there!
Far beyond this world of care;
When this troubled life shall cease,
Meet me where is perfect peace;
Where our sorrows we lay down
For the Kingdom and the crown
Jesus does a home prepare -
Meet me there! yes - meet me there!

Meet me there! Oh, meet me there!
No bereavements we shall bear;
There no signings for the dead,
There no farewell tear is shed;
We shall, safe from all alarms,
Clasp our loved ones in our arms,
And in Jesus glory share -
Meet me there! yes - meet me there!

Acknowledgements

In compiling a book such as this, the task of researching historical detail plays a very large part. I would like to pass on my sincere thanks to the following for their kind help in provision of archive material on the life of Rev. Wm. P. Nicholson.

To Rev. Stanley Barnes and Rev. Harry Scott whose supply of The Life of Faith articles gave the incentive to get started. My thanks especially to Rev. Barnes for all his encouragement throughout the project - for all his help with newspaper cuttings, books and photographs. His kindness was much appreciated.

To the Chittick family, Lisburn, who willingly gave consent to the use of the personal letters of Rev. Wm. P. Nicholson, Belfast Telegraph Library Archives for permission to reproduce newspaper reports.

To Mr. Ian Kinnard, Groomsport, for the Family Album photographs and others throughout the book. Mr. Robert Childs, Harland & Wolff for re-production of the 'Galgorm Castle', the 'Mauritania', and Island-men, the Y.M.C.A. Belfast for use of their historical pictures.

Thanks also to the following for use of material Mr. Ken McFall, (Carrickfergus Missions) Mr. Denzil McIlfatrick for his personal testimony, Rev. Ian R. K. Paisley for reproduction of his recollections and Irish Alliance of Christian Workers' Unions for archive publications.

Others who willingly supplied their 'keepsakes' of the Nicholson years - Mrs. Irene McDermott, (Coleraine) Mrs. Peggy Edgar, (Ballynahinch) Mrs. Helen McCune (Hillsborough) T. B. F. Thompson Ministries.

Thanks also to South Eastern Education & Library Board (Ballynahinch and Lisburn), Irish Linen Centre/Lisburn Museum for research facilities, and Trevor Hall for photographic services. Also others who offered possible sources of information whether used or not, provided transport, or helped in any way. Their assistance was very necessary and much appreciated.

A special thank you to my friend Mrs. Isabel McComb for her faithful prayer support.

And finally, thanks to Mr. Sam Lowry and staff of Ambassador Productions Ltd. for kindly undertaking publication of 'To God Be The Glory'.

Photograph Sources:

Alliance News Archives (I.A.C.W.U. Magazine)
Barnes, Stanley – *All for Jesus*
Belfast Telegraph Newspaper Archives
Cobain, Rev. R. – *Introducing Our Church*
County Down Spectator Archives
Eileen McAuley, Ballymoney
Every Home Crusade
From Civil War to Revival Victory
Gallagher, Rev. Eric – *At the Point of Need (Grosvenor Hall)*
Govan I. R. (Faith Mission) - *Spirit of Revival*
Hamilton Road Presbyterian Church (copy of funeral cortege)
Ian Kinnaird, Groomsport
Irish Linen Centre/Lisburn Museum
Jess, Ivan T. Ravenhill Presbyterian Church 1898-1998 Centenary History
John Chapman, Lisburn
Mavis Heaney
Maxwell, Victor – *Belfast's Halls of Faith and Fame*
McClean, J.B. –Victory a Triumph of Faith (Bangor Convention Souvenir Booklet)
McRostie, Ena – The Man who Walked Backwards
North Down Heritage Society
Paisley, Ian R. K. – *Tornado of the Pulpit*
Railway Street Presbyterian Church, Lisburn
Rev. Stanley Barnes
T. B. F. Thompson Ministries
Thompson, T. B. F. – *One Move Ahead*
Weir, W. Kenneth – *The House on Windmill Hill*

Bibliography:

Alliance News (I.A.C.W.U. Magazine)
Barnes, Stanley *All for Jesus*
Belfast Telegraph Library Archives
Bright Words Magazine (Faith Mission)
British Library Reproductions, 96 Euston Road, London NW1 2DB
Church of Ireland Gazette
County Down Spectator Library Archives
Glad Tidings (I.A.C.W.U. Magazine)
Irish Christian Advocate (1922)
Jess, Ivan T. – *Ravenhill Presbyterian Church
        1898 – 1998 Centenary History*
Long, Canon E. – *W. P. Nicholson 'The Rude Evangelist'*
McFall, Ken - *A Local Perspective – W. P. Nicholson*
        (foreword by Rev. Tom Shaw)
Murray. S. W. – *Flame for God in Ulster*
On Towards the Goal (Nicholson)
Paisley, Ian R. K. - *Nicholson – 1876 Centenary 1976*
Sacred Songs & Solos – *(Hymn: Meet Me There)*
The Leader Newspaper Archives
The Life of Faith Magazine (1950s)
The Lisburn Standard Newspaper Archives
Weir, Kenneth - *Greater Things Than These*

"If my experiences have been any encouragement or help to any, I have been well rewarded. I hope all have marvelled and wondered at the grace of God that could stoop so low and lift so little, and use me in His service.

Truly it is said, "Not many wise men after the flesh are called. But God hath chosen the foolish, the weak, the base, the despised, the nothings, that no flesh should glory in His presence." The world has yet to see what God can do for, and with, a man providing he won't touch the glory."

Rev. Wm. P. Nicholson Jno.3.30